PRAISE FOR *THE SEVEN LAWS OF LOVE*

Dave Willis is writing about the most important topic of all—love. It's literally what matters most. And he does a masterful job of showing us not only how it works, but how we can live it out in our real-life relationships. *The Seven Laws of Love* is insightful, compelling, inspiring, grounded, and immeasurably practical. We love this book! Everyone needs to read it. Don't miss out on its powerful message.

> —Drs. Les and Leslie Parrott, authors of *Saving Your Marriage Before It Starts*

Great marriages are never accidental. It took me years as a husband to learn that. Don't wait as long as I did. Get this book and get intentional. Dave Willis will show you how!

> —Jon Acuff, *New York Times* bestselling author of *Do Over* and *Stuff Christians Like*

The Seven Laws of Love is clear; concise; and fortunately for me, simple to understand and apply. I wish I'd written it myself. So does my wife.

> —Nathan Whitaker, #1 *New York Times* bestselling author

I wish I'd read Dave Willis's book before the first of my three marriages. I can testify that marriage is the bedrock of our culture. Once you get that wrong, it's hard to recover. This book is full of tips, encouragement, and biblical principles to help before you get hitched or once you made that hopefully life-long decision.

> —Stacey Dash, actress and Fox News contributor

If you want to be a better spouse, sibling, parent or friend, read this book! *The Seven Laws of Love* will give you a framework for building stronger, healthier relationships.

> —Dale Partridge, *Wall Street Journal* bestselling author of *People Over Profit*

One of the biggest needs in today's culture is to recapture the true depth, definition, and density of love. We've turned it into a fuzzy, emotional, Disney-esque thing, when in fact it's so much deeper and richer than that. Love is covenantal. It's our deepest desire, need, and longing. What I love most about Dave is he's relentless in pointing us back to that definition of love. One that fills us up, and lasts. I'm thankful for him and his words!

—Jefferson Bethke, *New York Times* bestselling author

Dave Willis is a servant leader with a gift of teaching and writing that connects and relates with people from all walks, ages, and stages of life. In *The Seven Laws of Love* he connects the reader with the scriptural foundations that every relationship needs in order to thrive. His insight and engaging writing style brings you into the moment of the stories shared to illustrate the vital principles for healthy relationships. Whether you are a husband, wife, parent, child, brother, sister or friend, *The Seven Laws of Love* should be on your must-read list for happier and healthier relationships.

—Wade Jackson, executive director, Family Dynamics Institute

Over the last few years, I've had the privilege of meeting and learning from Dave Willis. After sixteen years of marriage, I thought I had the "important" parts figured out. Through Dave's writings on his blog, and now this book, I've learned what it takes to build a stronger marriage. There are many who claim to be experts, but Dave defines what an expert is through how he lives—and then teaches others. This book is just one more example, and a blueprint you can use to build a strong and lasting marriage.

—Kimanzi Constable, author of the *Publishers Weekly*, iBooks, and Amazon #1 bestselling book *Are You Living or Existing? 9 Steps to Change Your Life*

Even though Catherine and I didn't come to our relationship in a very traditional way, I want to make sure I spend a lifetime with the woman I love. We're still newlyweds, but I know that marriage won't always be easy—that's where Dave Willis comes in. With practical and biblical advice, he sheds light on the ways that marriage can work well . . . and the ways we can accidentally mess it up. It's a complicated world out there, and this book provides a plan to navigate it well and for a lifetime!

—Sean Lowe, Star of ABC's *The Bachelor* and *New York Times* bestselling author of *For the Right Reasons*

Dave and his wife, Ashley, have powerful insight into the challenging dynamics of marriage. They had a major impact on the couples in our congregation when they led an iVow Marriage Conference at our church, and today we continue to use their writings as a foundation for ministry to couples and families. On a personal level, I can honestly say that Dave's influence has not only made me a better husband, but a better follower of Jesus. Whether you're celebrating fifty amazing years with your spouse; you're a newlywed just strapping into the roller coaster ride of your life; or you happen to be walking through crisis, chaos, and confusion in your marriage, *The Seven Laws of Love* will be a great resource for you.

—Anthony Braswell, lead pastor, Northpark Church

Dave's book is one of the most practical guides to love and relationships I've ever read. Every member of your family could benefit from *The Seven Laws of Love*.

—Craig Gross, founder of XXXchurch.com and author of *Go Small*

Dave is a prolific writer, a great preacher, and a friend. I have been impressed with his work as associate pastor at Steven's Creek Church in Augusta, Georgia, and I know Dave's ministry has impacted countless marriages and families. You will be blessed by his book.

—Bob Russell, retired senior minister, Southeast Christian Church

Dave Willis gets it. In today's chaotic world it takes a special blend of practical advice coupled with timeless God-given guidance to help marriages thrive. Dave delivers this gift in a profound way in *The Seven Laws of Love.*

—Dustin Riechmann, founder of EngagedMarriage. com and author of *15-Minute Marriage Makeover*

Dave is a gifted communicator. He writes and speaks in an easy-to-follow, yet helpful way. He combines humor with impact. He motivates his audience to action.

—Ron Edmondson, pastor, RonEdmondson.com

Dave gives hope to marriage with practical tips and tools that any couple can use to have an amazing marriage. Marriage and families are worth saving, and, if you are willing to take action, this process could be a marriage saver.

—Tony DiLorenzo, founder of ONE Extraordinary Marriage and cohost of the #1 marriage podcast on iTunes

Dave is a passionate advocate to help marriages thrive through positive encouragement and engaging challenges. Through his willingness to share personal stories from his life experience as a husband, father, friend, and pastor, Dave continues to inspire people to rely on God's truth and the design of marriage.

—Aaron and Jennifer Smith, founders of Husbandrevolution.com and Unveiledwife.com

In his new book, Dave Willis lays out seven simple but marriage-changing laws of love. Whether you're newlyweds or have been married long enough to finish each others' sentences, this light, fun book will challenge the way you look at your spouse and make the rest of your happily-ever-after even happier.

—Nancy French, *New York Times* bestselling author

Blending scripture, stories, and practical suggestions, *The Seven Laws of Love* teaches us what love is, and how to do it well. Applying Dave's wisdom will improve the way you love God, your spouse, your children, your friends, and yourself. A great book for anyone trying to be more generous.

—Paul H. Byerly, marriage and sex educator, creator of www.the-generous-husband.com, thexycode. com, and site.themarriagebed.com

Dave Willis's wisdom has helped me and countless numbers of people grow in their personal, family, and spiritual lives. Dave is a master story-teller. Get ready to learn something about yourself and how to be better at loving other people. *The Seven Laws of Love* offers practical ideas to help you build stronger relationships. You will be inspired and encouraged by the valuable insights in this book.

—Dr. Marty Baker, lead pastor of Stevens Creek Church and founder of SecureGive.com

I count it a privilege to endorse *The Seven Laws of Love.* Drawing heavily from his own personal and professional life, Dave interweaves today's real-life lessons with biblical stories in an extraordinary manner. You will love this book. All fourteen chapters are presented in a heart-gripping manner that leaves the reader with an increased knowledge of the Word, a keen appreciation for the beauty of life, and an inspiration to live every day in the fullness of the God's love.

—Mark L. Williams, general overseer, Church of God, Cleveland, Tennessee

Dave's book is easy to read, practical, and applicable in any relationship. Each chapter presents a real-life story that is relatable and life-changing. If you are looking to enhance your relationships and / or mend a broken heart, I highly recommend you read and apply *The Seven Laws of Love* in your life.

—Pardon Ndhlovu, 2016 Olympic marathon qualifier for Team Zimbabwe

THE
SEVEN
LAWS
OF LOVE

THE
SEVEN
LAWS
OF LOVE

ESSENTIAL PRINCIPLES FOR
BUILDING STRONGER RELATIONSHIPS

DAVE WILLIS

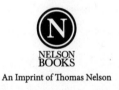

NELSON
BOOKS

An Imprint of Thomas Nelson

Published in Nashville, Tennessee, by Nelson Books, an imprint of Thomas Nelson. Nelson Books and Thomas Nelson are registered trademarks of HarperCollins Christian Publishing, Inc.

The author is represented by MacGregor Literary, Inc.

Thomas Nelson titles may be purchased in bulk for educational, business, fund-raising, or sales promotional use. For information, please e-mail SpecialMarkets@ThomasNelson.com.

Any Internet addresses, phone numbers, or company or product information printed in this book are offered as a resource and are not intended in any way to be or to imply an endorsement by Thomas Nelson, nor does Thomas Nelson vouch for the existence, content, or services of these sites, phone numbers, companies, or products beyond the life of this book.

Unless otherwise indicated, all Scripture quotations are taken from the *Holy Bible*, New Living Translation, copyright © 1996, 2004, 2007, 2013 by Tyndale House Foundation. Used by permission of Tyndale House Publishers, Inc., Carol Stream, Illinois 60188. All rights reserved.

Scripture quotations marked NIV are taken from THE HOLY BIBLE, NEW INTERNATIONAL VERSION®, NIV® Copyright © 1973, 1978, 1984, 2011 by Biblica, Inc.® Used by permission. All rights reserved worldwide.

Scripture quotations marked KJV are from The Holy Bible, King James Version.

Library of Congress Cataloging-in-Publication Data

Willis, Dave, 1978-
 The seven laws of love : essential principles for building stronger relationships / Dave Willis.
   pages cm
 ISBN 978-0-7180-3433-7
 1. Love--Religious aspects--Christianity. I. Title. II. Title: Seven laws of love.
 BV4639.W487 2016
 241'.4--dc23

                                                        2015002185

Printed in the United States of America

15 16 17 18 19 RRD 6 5 4 3 2 1

To Ashley, your love inspires me every day.

CONTENTS

FOREWORD

Not long ago, I was sitting beside my mom in the hospital. Just a few days before, my vigorous and active 72-year-old father had had a massive middle-of-the-night stroke. My parents have been inseparable for nearly fifty years of marriage, and so they were in this. Despite her own exhaustion, my mother slept by his hospital bed every night and rarely left his side.

Quietly she began to tell me more of the story: the sudden awakening as she felt my dad collapse against her; her alarm as she realized he couldn't move or speak; fighting the clock to get him help before there was too much irreparable brain damage; her worry and her prayers as they whisked him away in the emergency room and she was not allowed to follow; the long minutes staring at the swinging doors to the medical area, wondering what the news would be when they opened again.

"You must have been so scared!" I said.

My mom looked up at me with tears in her eyes. "It was a long wait. But the whole time, all I could think was that if this was it, I was so incredibly grateful for the time we have been given."

Why do tears form in *my* eyes as I write those words? Why do we get secretly choked up when we read the story of the husband and wife married sixty-five years, who placed their beds in the nursing home side by side and held hands every night until they passed on within days of each other? Why do we feel emotion stirring when we hear of a total stranger putting their life on the line for another? Or even when we see someone reach out to comfort a hurting friend at just the right time?

It is because we all recognize true love when we see it—and something in every one of us longs for it.

No matter what has happened in our lives, no matter what hurts or joys, something in every human heart wants to be a part of that kind of story. To not only receive true love, but to give it. To be a conduit for it.

We recognize true love when we see it—but we don't always know how to replicate it. What does it mean to truly love others like that, and to experience that love in return? You may ask: What if I don't feel worthy of that love? What if I don't believe it is even possible in my life? You may wonder: Can I even *hope* to experience so much love in my life that I come to a point where I can truthfully say I was just so thankful for the time we were given?

Yes. You can.

Dave Willis has written a remarkable book to lead you down the path to experiencing that sort of true love—whether that is as a friend, a neighbor, a spouse, a parent, or a follower of the Author of Love. And the insights in this book are remarkable, because God has given Dave a remarkable amount of wisdom.

Very few books on my shelf are "pen-worthy" like this one.

For some reason, I really don't like marking up books as I read; I like having fresh, clean pages in front of me. But every now and then I simply can't help but grab a pen and start underlining, or start marking passages on my e-reader.

You should see the number of markings on my copy of this book. So many truths that I want to pull out and chew on, over and over again—so many ways that I want to look like this love Dave outlines:

- "A life of love requires that we look in the mirror and give an honest and humble self-assessment."
- "You don't have to trust someone in order to forgive, but you do have to forgive someone in order to make trust possible again."
- "Your character should always be stronger than your circumstances."
- "A husband and wife must operate like two wings on the same bird; if they don't work together in full partnership, the marriage will never get off the ground. Trust makes that possible [while] secrecy is the enemy of intimacy."
- "Time is the currency of relationships, so consistently invest time in your marriage."
- "Being nice to people isn't a personality trait; it's a choice."
- "When you step from his life into eternity, love will be all that matters."

Those are my challenges, my needs to work on, my truths that I want to remember in order to be a person of love.

What are yours? Get out your pen, my friends. Very soon, you'll be marking up this copy of *The Seven Laws of Love*.

Let's aspire together to be people of love.

—Shaunti Feldhahn

Social researcher and bestselling author
of *For Women Only* and *For Men Only*

INTRODUCTION
Love Defined

If I could speak all the languages of earth and of angels, but didn't love others, I would only be a noisy gong or a clanging cymbal. If I had the gift of prophecy, and if I understood all of God's secret plans and possessed all knowledge, and if I had such faith that I could move mountains, but didn't love others, I would be nothing. If I gave everything I have to the poor and even sacrificed my body, I could boast about it; but if I didn't love others, I would have gained nothing.

—1 CORINTHIANS 13:1–3

L ove is the most powerful force on earth.

I recently visited a place where the life-changing power of love was evident everywhere I looked, an orphanage in Guatemala called Casa Shalom. The name means "House of Peace," and it truly is a place of peace and love for the nearly one hundred precious kids who call it home.

My friends Josh and Jessica are investing their lives into leading this orphanage while simultaneously raising their own young family. In the midst of all this, Jessica has courageously fought and won a battle against cancer. They're a heroic couple, and, undoubtedly, their ongoing legacy of love will shape countless lives for generations to come.

As Josh gave our missions team a tour of the property, he told us the story of how each child came to be there. "There goes Eduardo. His parents were killed by drug dealers. That's Rosa. She and her brothers were living on the streets before they were brought here. They were eating out of trash cans and severely malnourished."

Each child had a story, and most of those stories were heartbreaking. Despite the brokenness of their home situations, these children seemed so happy and healthy. Josh knew each one by name, and he beamed like a proud papa as he hugged the kids and bragged about how they were great at soccer or art or singing.

At one point a teenage girl walked up and gave Josh a hug, and as she skipped away, Josh had tears in his eyes. He began to tell me her story. "Her name is Margerita," he said. "She grew up in a home with horrific abuse. Her father was a drunk, and he abused her in the worst kinds of ways. She was eventually taken out of that home and placed in a home with her aunt and uncle, but her uncle abused her in the same terrible ways that her father had done. She stayed in several more homes, but in each situation the very people who should have been protecting her abused her. When she finally came here, she was brokenhearted and alone. She didn't trust anyone. She barely spoke. We weren't sure if we'd ever get through to her. We kept praying for her and doing our best to show her God's love in meaningful ways, but after several months of trying, nothing seemed to be working."

Josh paused to wipe some tears from his eyes as he continued the story. "One night, Jessica and I were sitting on the hillside watching the sunset like we do most nights. We were watching the boys play soccer and the girls jump rope, taking in all the beautiful sights and sounds of Casa Shalom. Then Margerita came and sat down. She had always kept her distance, especially from men. But she scooted right next to me, and what she did next completely took my breath away. She rested her head on my shoulder. I held my breath, waiting for her to speak. When she finally looked up at me, she spoke some words that I'll never forget."

NOW I KNOW I'M SAFE HERE. AND I BELIEVE THAT YOU REALLY LOVE ME.

At this point, I was leaned in so far that *my* head was practically on his shoulder in anticipation. He gathered his composure, and with a smile on his face, he relived that beautiful moment. "She looked up at me and said, 'When I first came here, I never believed I would ever be safe, and I never believed anyone would ever really love me. But now I know I'm safe here. And I believe that you really love me.'"

That became a life-changing moment for Josh, a beautiful picture of what love really means. The way God loves us and the way Josh and Jessica love Margerita (and every child at Casa Shalom*) shows us how love is supposed to look. Love brought healing to Margerita's broken heart.

When we experience real love, it always has the power to bring healing and transformation. As love takes root, our lives and the lives of our loved ones will be dramatically changed.

---

* To learn more about the Casa Shalom orphanage, visit www.CasaShalom.net.

THE POINT OF LIFE

In our fast-paced culture, we're all tempted to chase stuff that doesn't matter. We're conditioned to value possessions over people, but people must always take priority over all other pursuits. I firmly believe that God created love to be the centerpiece of life. There's no higher purpose on earth than to love and be loved.

My mom was a hospice nurse for many years, and, as a kid, I would tag along with her on some of her home visits. Hanging out with people who were dying forever changed my perspective on love and life. I discovered that when a person knows his or her time on earth is short, what matters most comes into focus more clearly than ever before.

For these dying patients, whether they were young or old, black or white, male or female, educated or illiterate, their priorities at the end of life were remarkably similar: faith, families, and friendships. Their relationships were all that mattered. In short, they cared about love. Every joy they treasured in those final moments was related to love, and every regret that tormented them was tied to a failure to give or receive love.

LIVING WELL STARTS WITH LOVING WELL.

The key to a purpose-filled, regret-free life starts with a deeper understanding of love. Living well starts with loving well.

LOVE LESSONS

Love can make us do crazy things. I have a long list of love-fueled crazy choices I've made in my life. One item on that list would be my decision to coach my son Cooper's basketball team when he was five years old. I knew almost nothing about basketball. I played pickup games in my school days, but my lack of height, nonexistent vertical-leaping ability, and prominent love handles made me a less-than-ideal draft pick for the sport.

In addition to my very limited knowledge, I also had no expertise in herding five-year-olds. You've got to have a lot of love and a ridiculous amount of patience to teach kids at that age. (When you kindergarten teachers get to heaven, you'll definitely be the ones living in the gated community.)

I was fearful about coaching, but my apprehension was outweighed by my love for my son. Love is powerful, so when you pit your love against your fear, love will win every time. Cooper wanted me to coach, and I looked into those puppy-dog eyes and said, "Sure, buddy! I'd love to coach your team!"

I had high hopes of turning those energetic whippersnappers into future Olympians, but I quickly learned that we needed to start with the basics: dribbling the ball instead of running with it, not hugging other players during the game, not hugging the referees during the game, and keeping the ball inbounds.

Surprisingly, of all the lessons I attempted to teach them, the concept of keeping the ball inbounds proved to be the toughest lesson for them to grasp.

At first, the white outlines around the court were meaningless to the kids. Once they started bouncing the ball, they just kept going with no regard for the boundary lines. They also didn't seem to be able to hear me blowing the whistle and shouting for them to stop. They would often end up outside the gym before I could get to them. Five-year-olds are much faster than they look.

Midway through the season, the concept of boundaries finally clicked, and that's when the real basketball actually started. Until they learned to keep the ball inbounds, no matter how fast they ran or how hard they played, it didn't matter. If it wasn't inbounds, it didn't count.

Love is the same way. Love creates the boundaries of life. They aren't always as easy to see, but they are just as important. Everything we do within love makes a difference, and everything we do outside of love doesn't really matter in the end.

When God created us, he told us plainly what's most important: "The only thing that counts is faith expressing itself through love" (Gal. 5:6 NIV).

LOVE IS THE ONLY PART OF LIFE THAT REALLY COUNTS.

In essence, love is the only part of life that really counts. The love you have for God and for your family and friends will shape your life and future. Our careers and our looks and our golf games will all someday fall apart, but love has the power to stand the test of time. A life out of love is a life out of bounds.

THE BOUNDARY LINES OF LOVE

Love creates the boundary lines for life, but what creates the boundary lines for love?

Just like ignoring the double yellow lines on a highway, if you choose to consistently disregard the boundaries, eventually you will cause great harm to yourself and others. The trouble is that the boundary lines of love aren't as clearly seen as the glow-in-the-dark yellow paint on the highway. They're harder to see, but they're even more important.

Maybe you're apprehensive about words like *boundaries* or *laws* associated with love, because you've always believed love is free and uncontainable. In some ways, you're right. God did create love to be limitless and eternal, like an ocean with an unreachable depth, but he also created parameters for how this extraordinary gift of love must be given and received.

My friend Tommy shared an insight that illustrates this whole idea of boundaries with more clarity. He told me that the Mississippi River and the Florida Everglades have approximately the same amount of water flowing through them, but they look drastically different. The Mississippi River provides transport to people and cargo and also enriches the soil on all sides of it, making the Mississippi Delta some of the most fertile soil anywhere.

The Everglades, by contrast, is a treacherous place. The swampy topography makes any travel or farming almost impossible. It's also a place where you're fairly likely to encounter some unwelcoming alligators.

The only real difference between the Everglades and the Mississippi River is the fact that the river has banks. Those banks provide boundaries that funnel and focus the power of the river. Conversely, the lack of boundary lines for the Everglades' water flow creates an uninhabitable, swampy mess.

God wants love to flow through our lives like a mighty river. The Laws of Love are the invisible banks God has placed around love for our prosperity and protection. When our relationships live within those boundaries, everyone involved is enriched. When we dismiss or disregard the boundaries, our relationships can quickly become unhealthy and unsustainable.

DEFINING *LOVE*

When Jesus was asked what mattered most, he answered: "'You must love the Lord your God with all your heart, all your soul, and all your mind.' This is the first and greatest commandment. A second is equally important: 'Love your neighbor as yourself.' The entire law and all the demands of the prophets are based on these two commandments" (Matt. 22:37–40).

Love God and love people. It's that simple. Even the Beatles famously sang, "Love is all you need!"

A couple years ago, my wife, Ashley, bought tickets for us to see comedian Jerry Seinfeld as a birthday gift for me. I've always been a fan of Seinfeld's comedy, because he masterfully takes mundane details of daily life and helps us see them with a new perspective and a funny twist.

Jerry told jokes that night about Pop-Tarts and parenthood. He pointed out that most of our body heat escapes through the head. Pondering this further, he said, "I suppose that means you could go snow skiing naked if you had a really good hat."

We have more than body heat escaping through our heads, though. We tend to see love only as a matter of the heart, primarily an issue of feelings over facts. But when we remove our brains from the equation, as we are sometimes prone to do, our capacity to give and receive love can escape right through our heads.

GOD CREATED LOVE TO BE A MATTER OF BOTH THE HEART *AND* THE MIND.

God created love to be a matter of both the heart *and* the mind. Our feelings and emotions are part of the equation, but they're not the compasses we should trust to guide our actions. Feelings are fickle, and there's far too much at stake to just blindly follow our feelings.

If you asked one hundred different people to define love, you would probably end up with one hundred different definitions. This is obviously problematic, because if we're all defining love in different ways, then the true meaning of love is being lost in the process. For the sake of clarity and consistency, we need to look to the Bible, the original and authoritative text on matters of life and love.

After studying all that the Bible has to teach us about love, I've boiled down hundreds of love-related passages of Scripture into the following definition:

> Love is an unconditional commitment to selflessly serve, truthfully communicate, fearlessly protect, gracefully forgive, compassionately heal, and enduringly remain in relationship with and for the sake of another.

The Seven Laws of Love are wrapped up in this single definition. This is what love looks like, and the remainder of this book will be focused on how to bring its limitless power into your life and your relationships.

FOR THOSE WHO ARE HURTING

Maybe you're reading this book because your relationships are already strong and you want to help them grow even stronger. Perhaps you've made consistent investments into them like the investment of time you're making to read this. I applaud you and hope you find encouragement and valuable insight in the pages to come.

I also know that many who are reading this book have felt burned by love in the past. You're reading this with a broken heart. You have one or more relationships that have crumbled, and you're trying to make sense of it all. You're wrestling with a mixture of pain, grief, regret, confusion, frustration, and maybe even bitterness.

I don't know your exact situation, but I believe you're not reading this book by accident. I believe in a God who works all things together for good, and I believe his love has the power to bring healing to anything we could ever face. He cares about you. He is present in your moments of heartache. I recently heard a story that beautifully illustrates God's love for the brokenhearted:

> A woman who had fifteen children was once asked, "With so many kids, how do you love them all the same?"
>
> She smiled and gave an unexpected reply: "I don't love them all the same. The one who is hurting the most, the one who feels the most loneliness, the one who is broken-hearted . . . that's the one I love the most."

God has a lot more kids than just fifteen, and I don't believe that he plays favorites. But the Bible does teach that God has a special place in his heart for those who are hurting. He's with us always, but in our moments of deepest despair, I believe his presence is strongest.

"The LORD is close to the brokenhearted; he rescues those whose spirits are crushed" (Ps. 34:18).

If you are in a place right now where you feel all alone in your search for real love, I want to reassure you that you are not alone. God hasn't forgotten about you. He loves you with an eternal love, and he will never abandon you. No matter where you've been, what you've done, or what's been done to you, God has a love-filled, redemptive plan for you.

EVERYBODY QUALIFIES

Love is what motivated my Great Uncle Joe to get out of his bed at midnight almost thirty years ago. He leaned over to his wife and told her that he had to go do something. He felt strongly that God had given him an important assignment, and it couldn't wait until morning. It seemed like a crazy mission, but he knew in his gut that it had to be done right away.

She was way too tired to argue or ask many questions, so he kissed her on the forehead, put on a jacket over his pajamas, and walked out to his truck. He drove to the outskirts of their little Indiana farm town and pulled into the parking lot of a place he'd driven past a thousand times but had never gone inside. The sign read, "Welcome to the Red Fox Bar."

The Red Fox was infamous for the brawlers, strippers, and scoundrels who frequented the place. The man who owned and tended the bar was a legendary wild man named Jughead. His real name was Leon, but everyone called him Jughead or Jug for short. No one seemed sure where or how the nickname had originated, but it seemed to fit him well.

Jug looked up from the bar and saw my Uncle Joe walking in wearing his pj's and house slippers. Uncle Joe was a preacher and never had much use for alcohol, so the bartender had to do a double take to be sure of what he was seeing. He finally shook his head and laughed out loud. "Well, I never! What are you doing in here, preacher man? What can I pour you to drink?"

"Hey, Jug," Uncle Joe replied with a yawn. "I'm not here for a drink."

"Well, you do realize it's a bar, don't you? If you're not here for a drink, then what on earth are you here for?"

Uncle Joe walked up to the bar and said, "This has never happened to me before, but I believe God woke me up tonight and gave me a very specific assignment. He wanted me to drive down here and give you a message."

Jug exploded with laughter and smacked the bar with amused delight. "Oh, God has a message for me, does he? I'll bet he does! You Christians are always telling me about God's message for me. What is it this time? Are you here to tell me that I'm going to hell for running a bar or that my wife's going to hell because she used to be a stripper? Does God want me to know that I'm worthless? I heard that message my entire childhood from my dad, so I certainly don't need to hear it again. So tell me, preacher, what is God's message for me?"

Uncle Joe put his hands down on the bar and looked Jug in the eyes. And with a piercing conviction and compassion in his voice, he said, "Jug, God wanted me to tell you that he loves you and he has an extraordinary plan for your life."

Jug immediately looked down at the bar and began wiping it off with a towel as if Uncle Joe were invisible. Joe turned to walk back outside, thinking his assignment was complete and he could go back to bed. But before he got to the exit, he heard Jug's voice.

"Wait!"

Uncle Joe turned around, and Jug was standing behind the bar with tears streaming down his face. With a quiver in his voice, he asked, "Is that true? Does God really love me? Nobody has ever told me that before."

Uncle Joe walked back to the bar and sat down. The two men talked and laughed and cried until the early hours of the morning. Jug prayed the first prayer of his life at that bar, and he asked God to forgive him of his sins and committed to living the rest of his life following Jesus, embracing God's limitless love, and sharing that love with others. Right there at the bar that night, love changed Jug's life forever.

Jug put a "For Sale" sign out in front of the Red Fox and refused to sell the building to anyone who would continue using it as a bar. He walked away from his old life and wholeheartedly embraced a new one. His personal transformation caused such a stir in the small town that a revival broke out, beginning with his wife (the retired stripper) and many of the patrons of the bar. Jug eventually became a preacher, and today he continues to live out his promise of living a life of love and grace and helping others to do the same.

ONCE PEOPLE REALIZE THAT THEY'RE TRULY, FULLY, UNCONDITIONALLY LOVED, IT CHANGES EVERYTHING.

I love this story, because it's a reminder of the infinite power of love. Once people realize that they're truly, fully, unconditionally loved, it changes everything. Maybe you've forgotten, or maybe, like Jug, you've never been told, but God loves you, and he has an extraordinary plan for your life. He wants you to live a life of love.

I pray that God will use this book to help you experience the fullness and beauty of real love in new and profound ways. I hope the journey will expand your capacity to give and receive love and equip you with the tools to do both. I believe you're at the beginning of a new chapter of renewal and restoration in your relationships that has the potential to change your life and the lives of those you love. Thank you for allowing me the privilege of being a small part of your journey.

Let's get started!

PART ONE

THE
LAWS
OF LOVE

CHAPTER 1

LOVE REQUIRES COMMITMENT

Love never gives up, never loses faith, is always hopeful,
and endures through every circumstance.

—1 CORINTHIANS 13:7

I *love you.*

These three little words make up the most significant phrase you could ever speak and the most beautiful phrase you could ever hear. These are the words we say to our newborn babies the moment we first hold them in our arms. They're the words people utter to friends and family members from their deathbeds. They're the words we use to signify a new level of commitment in romantic relationships. They're the words God is speaking to us through every page of Scripture, every new sunrise, and every act of beauty and grace. These three little words are packed with power!

I vividly remember the first time I spoke these words to my wife, Ashley.

To accurately paint the picture of this scene, you need to know it was one of the least romantic places imaginable. My college dorm room was dingy and dirty. To my knowledge, my roommate hadn't washed his sheets even once in the two years I'd been living with him. We constantly sprayed Febreze and Lysol, but our best efforts to mask the stench of dirty clothes, wet towels, and old food did little to create much ambience. My sweet mom nearly cried the first time she visited.

As unpleasant as the surroundings may have been, all those unsavory details seemed to disappear when I looked at Ashley. I had never felt that way about anyone, and I figured it had to be love. I had to tell her. It felt like a volcano of unexpressed emotion was welling up in my heart and trying to come out of my mouth. I knew that if I didn't say something right then, there was a decent chance I'd end up puking on her instead. This was a defining moment.

The look on my face must have been a combination of nausea, fear, anticipation, confusion, and joy. Ashley gave me a concerned look with those gorgeous eyes of hers and said, "What are you thinking about?"

I felt completely vulnerable and exposed, like I was standing in my underwear in front of everyone I knew—and just to be clear, I've never looked very attractive in my underwear. (The more of my body I can cover up, the more attractive it seems.)

My mouth was dry, and I was having trouble forming coherent words, but I swallowed hard and gathered my strength. And with the squeaky voice of a prepubescent adolescent, I finally said, "I was thinking . . . I was thinking that I love you."

I got it out. It was not one of my smoothest moments, and I doubt the scene will ever be replayed in a great love story, but I got it out. I said it. She smiled at me, and without hesitation she said, "I love you too."

Even though we were still in my nasty dorm room, in that moment we might as well have been on top of the Eiffel Tower with fireworks going off in the background. I had expressed my love, and that love had been reciprocated. It's amazing how free and how strong you can feel when you know you're loved.

IT'S AMAZING HOW FREE AND HOW STRONG YOU CAN FEEL WHEN YOU KNOW YOU'RE LOVED.

Through our years together and the different seasons of our marriage and family, our love has grown deeper and richer. We've also gained a fuller understanding of what love really means. It's not something that can be defined by feelings or captured by words alone. God created love to be a transformative force in every aspect of our lives, and once we understand and embrace it, our lives come into clearer focus and our relationships grow in deeper levels of intimacy. Everything changes for the better.

Before that can happen, though, there must be commitment. Without a real commitment, there can be no real love.

THE FOUNDATION OF A STRONG RELATIONSHIP

My kids have an ongoing project of building a fort in the empty lot next to our house. Almost every day after school, they'll meet up with the other neighborhood kids and look for scrap materials to add to their beloved masterpiece. It's really nothing more than some old crates and cardboard stacked together.

Every time a storm comes, the whole thing falls apart, and they have to start the whole process over again.

I've never been much help on the fort project because I'm terrible with tools. Ashley's dad is a guy who can build and fix anything, so when Ashley married me, she assumed all men had the same skill set. I wish I had those skills, but when I try swinging a hammer, stuff gets broken. Ashley is both the beautiful one and the handy one in our relationship.

The boys wish I were better at construction so I could help them build the fort. I do my best to help them gather materials, but my most valuable contribution thus far has been a single bit of engineering advice. I told them the fort was going to keep collapsing until they built it securely on a solid foundation.

Many relationships resemble that fort. Maybe there's a lot of effort going into building the relationship, but it still seems to fall apart. Relationships can crumble because of a lack of effort, but in other cases the relationship fails for the same reasons the boys' fort kept collapsing. It's built with the wrong tools and with no solid foundation.

Matthew 7:24–27 contains one of Jesus' most famous teachings. He tells the story of a wise builder and a foolish builder. The wise builder took the time to build his house on a foundation of solid rock, while the foolish builder took the fast and easy route and built his house on sand.

THE STRENGTH OF YOUR COMMITMENT WILL ALWAYS DETERMINE THE STRENGTH OF YOUR RELATIONSHIP.

From the outside, both houses looked the same, but the difference was revealed when a storm came. The strong winds and rains beat against both houses, and the house without a solid foundation collapsed. The house built on the rock stood strong.

When you read magazines and look at the examples of love in pop culture, it seems as though many people are content to build a relationship with no solid foundation. These shaky relationships are usually based on fickle feelings, codependent insecurities, mutual convenience, or lust. When the storms of life come, the relationships can't survive.

The strongest relationships, however, are built on a foundation of love, and love is always built on a solid foundation of commitment. The strength of your commitment will always determine the strength of your relationship.

THE COMMITMENT OF LOVE

God's definition of love and the first Law of Love is rooted in the concept of commitment. When you say "I love you" to someone, you aren't just expressing your current feelings; you're making a promise of commitment for your shared future.

Love, by its very nature, is a conscious choice to selflessly put the needs of someone else ahead of your own preferences or comforts. No relationship can survive unless it is rooted in rock-solid commitment.

As a pastor, I have the privilege of officiating wedding ceremonies. It's such an honor to stand in that sacred moment with a bride and groom as they exchange vows and rings and enter into the holy covenant of marriage. One of the Bible passages I often read at wedding ceremonies comes from the first chapter of the book of Ruth. It reads:

> But Ruth replied, "Don't ask me to leave you and turn back. Wherever you go, I will go; wherever you live, I will live. Your

people will be my people, and your God will be my God. Wherever you die, I will die, and there I will be buried. May the LORD punish me severely if I allow anything but death to separate us!" (Ruth 1:16–17).

These words beautifully capture the commitment necessary for a strong marriage, but I'm always quick to point out that these words weren't spoken in the context of marriage. In fact, this beautiful promise was spoken in a much unexpected way. The story gives us some fascinating insight into the power of commitment in all healthy relationships.

Ruth was a young Moabite woman who lived around three thousand years ago. Times were very difficult back then, and Ruth's young husband died. Based on the religious and cultural customs of the day, she no longer had any obligation to her husband's family, and she was free to pursue a new life. Though Ruth could do as she wished, she refused to leave her mother-in-law, Naomi.

Ruth knew Naomi had no one, and Ruth selflessly committed her life to Naomi's service. Because of Ruth's selflessness, God blessed her in remarkable ways. Not only did God provide food and shelter for the two women, but God brought a man named Boaz into Ruth's life.

This rich kinsman-redeemer married Ruth, and together they started a family. Their lineage became a generational line of love. Ruth and Boaz had a son named Obed who had a son named Jesse who had a son named David. David became the greatest king in Israel's history and the author of many of the Bible's psalms and poetry.

King David's lineage continued with a son named Solomon, who wrote the Wisdom Literature in the Bible and was blessed by God to be the wisest man of his day, but all this royalty was only the tip of the iceberg. God's ultimate plan through this family tree would happen a thousand years later.

Two descendants of King David named Joseph and Mary made their way to the City of David for a census. The town was called Bethlehem. Mary was expecting a child. She gave birth to a son named Jesus.

He was the son of God. He was the Prince of Peace. He was the embodiment of love.

God brought his own son through the lineage of a poor young woman named Ruth who understood the power of commitment and the meaning of love. God wants to create a generational impact through your life as well. The level at which you'll make an eternal impact is defined by your level of commitment to the people God has placed in your life.

COMMITMENT AND CONSISTENCY

Our commitment to others is evident in the consistency with which we serve them. Grand, one-time gestures can be nice, but it's what we do with consistency that will ultimately shape our relationships. I met a couple recently who reminded me of the power of consistency in a beautiful way.

Harold and Louise are an extraordinary couple. Ashley and I had the privilege of meeting them at a marriage conference we were hosting, and we were instantly drawn to them. There was a sparkle in their eyes and an adoration they obviously had for each other. They couldn't keep themselves from smiling every time their eyes met. Even though they were both in their seventies, they acted like two teenagers in love.

I spent as much time around them as I could that weekend because I wanted to learn the secret of their lifelong love. I wanted to know how their love had grown richer with time and how, even through painful setbacks in Louise's health, they both remained joyful, optimistic, and passionately devoted to each other. Louise is now confined to a wheelchair, but she looks like she could float on air when she looks at Harold.

Louise shared a story with us that gave us a glimpse into their relationship: "Our first date was on March 17, so on April 17, Harold brought me a long-stem rose to celebrate our one-month anniversary. I was genuinely impressed by his thoughtfulness, but I didn't expect the roses to come very often. I was so surprised when he brought me another rose on May 17 to celebrate our second month together. I smiled and thought, *Wow! This fella is a keeper!*"

She looked at Harold with a smile and continued her story. "After we got married, I expected the roses to stop, but on the seventeenth that first month of our marriage, another rose appeared."

She paused to squeeze Harold's hand, and tears began to form in her eyes as she smiled and said, "It has been fifty-four years since our first date, and every month on the seventeenth for 648 months in a row, Harold has brought me a rose."

> IT'S A SIMPLE CHOICE TO PUT LOVE INTO ACTION BY CONSISTENTLY SERVING, ENCOURAGING, SUPPORTING, AND ADORING EACH OTHER.

As she finished, I was simultaneously inspired by their love story and feeling like a jerk for having never done anything for Ashley that could match that level of consistent thoughtfulness. Harold definitely challenged me to raise the bar in my own marriage! I obviously couldn't build a time machine and go back to the beginning to start that type of tradition, but I can (and you can too) start today to bring more thoughtfulness and romance to the marriage.

Harold and Louise would be quick to tell you it takes a lot more than roses to build a strong, lifelong marriage. The flowers weren't really even the point of their story; it was the thoughtfulness behind the flowers. As I spend time with couples who have successfully loved each other for decades, I'm convinced their secret is really no secret at all. It's a simple choice to put love into action by consistently serving, encouraging, supporting, and adoring each other. Make those simple but powerful acts of love a priority in your relationships, and you'll be writing a happy ending to your own love stories.

OUR BIGGEST BARRIER TO COMMITMENT

One of the biggest emergencies in our modern relationship crisis is a widespread disregard for this first Law of Love. Our culture is suffering from a lack of real commitment. Many people seem to treat their relationships like possessions that can be upgraded or traded in for newer models. We trade in our cell phones every year or two, and many people trade in their relationships with the same frequency. This collective lack of commitment stems from a sense of entitlement for "On Demand" intimacy. Our modern culture has grown more impatient, and impatience is a massive barrier to commitment.

In order to become more committed, we need to become more patient. Love and patience may seem uncorrelated, but in God's design, patience is an ever-present attribute of love. The Bible teaches us love is patient, so we need to become more patient for love to take root in our relationships. Our relationships will thrive when we abandon the pull of instant gratification. Research backs me up on this.

In 1972, Stanford University conducted a groundbreaking study that unearthed a powerful insight into human behavior and relationships. The test was simple, but the results proved to be profound. Hundreds of children from all walks of life were brought onto campus and given what is now famously known as "The Marshmallow Test."*

The instructions were basic. Each child was asked to sit down at a table, and a researcher would place a marshmallow in front of the hungry kid and then give this proposition: "You can eat this marshmallow right now, but if you don't eat it right now and wait until I get back, I'll give you two marshmallows to eat."

They could have one now or two later. That was the test. Many kids would gobble up the marshmallow even before they heard the rules. Others would wait a little while, but eventually their willpower would disappear and they'd give in and eat it. A few kids found the inner strength to wait. They refused to settle for one marshmallow when patience would double the prize.

The kids who resisted the temptation didn't usually do it by willpower alone. They wouldn't just sit still and stare at the marshmallow. They got up and played and pretended the marshmallow wasn't even there until the researcher came back and gave them two. They beat temptation by removing the single marshmallow as an option, because they resolved that a better option was coming and it was well worth the wait.

This study was so valuable because the researchers followed those kids into adulthood and continued to measure their

---

* http://www.whatispsychology.biz/
deferred-gratification-stanford-marshmallow-experiment.

progress in different areas of their lives. They recorded profound differences between the "one marshmallow kids" and the "two marshmallow kids." The kids who had shown restraint and waited for two marshmallows were statistically much more likely to have a successful career, financial stability, and a long-term marriage.

In short, the study determined that the factor that was most likely to determine the lifelong health and happiness of an individual wasn't ethnicity, gender, family of origin, or even intelligence. The most important factor in determining the long-term health and vitality of a person's life and relationships was tied to one single discipline: the ability to delay gratification. In other words, patience is one of the most critical life skills a person can possess.

Intuitively, we know this to be true, and yet it can be so difficult to put into practice. I know that patience is important, but I've struggled with it all my life. I'd like to think I would have been a "two marshmallow kid," but I doubt I would have been. I catch myself watching the lines at Walmart and estimating which one will go the fastest, and if I end up choosing a line that moves slowly, I nearly have a panic attack. Then, if the person in line ahead of me pays with a check and tries to balance his or her checkbook while I'm waiting, I have to restrain myself from shouting, "Who pays with a check? What century do you live in?"

LOVE IS PATIENT, BUT WE STILL LIVE IN A VERY IMPATIENT WORLD.

I obviously have some ongoing struggles related to patience. It's a lifelong lesson I'm still trying to learn. (I apologize if you still pay for things using checks. I don't judge you, although I do encourage you to check out the amazing technology of debit cards. They'll change your life and make your Walmart checkout experience go much faster!)

Love is patient, but we still live in a very impatient world. We watch our shows On Demand. We have DVRs so we can fast-forward through commercials. We have express lanes at grocery stores so we don't get stuck behind someone with a cartful of groceries, and when someone gets in front of us in the express lane with too many items in his or her cart, we act like a felony has been committed. We hate traffic, long lines, waiting rooms, and anything or anyone who interrupts our agendas. In general, we're impatient, and we want everything right now! We live in a "one marshmallow now" society.

This On Demand mentality has swarmed into our relationships and threatened to replace the patience of love with the immediacy of pleasure. We're tempted to make compromises so that we can extract the positive feelings of love without the time and commitment love requires. In our impatience and selfishness, our culture has attempted to redefine love and has embraced some very damaging compromises in the process.

We've traded true intimacy for porn. We've traded committed marriages for commitment-free cohabitation. We've traded having children for having pets. We've traded meaningful conversations for text messages. We've traded "'til death do us part" for divorce. We've traded the pursuit of holiness for the pursuit of happiness. We've traded love for lust.

We've attempted to exploit all the benefits and pleasures of love without investing the commitment and self-sacrifice that love requires.

We can say we value love, but too often our actions prove we value other things much more. I'm saying this as a guy who has made many of the mistakes I've just outlined.

Once we become willing to choose the patient path of love, we'll be poised to take our relationships to a new level of healing and health. Love isn't a quick fix. Love is a lifelong pursuit. Commit to patiently applying the Laws of Love to your life, and over time you'll see a tremendous impact in the health of your relationships.

LOVE IS A LIFELONG PURSUIT.

NO EXIT STRATEGY

Love requires commitment, and commitment requires abandoning our exit strategies.

One of my favorite examples of removing any exit strategy comes from the prophet Elisha. The Old Testament book of 1 Kings chronicles Elisha's extraordinary story. God called Elisha into a life of ministry, but Elisha wisely understood that embracing his calling would mean letting go of his current career. He had to make a choice between his love for God and his need for the familiarity and financial security of his home.

Elisha was a farmer from a family of farmers. His cattle and his farming equipment represented his family trade, his heritage, and his income. Elisha didn't want the temptation of a comfortable exit strategy in his mind on the days when his new life in ministry might get uncomfortable. Elisha wanted to go all in with God.

To simultaneously celebrate his new calling and publicly display his commitment to God, Elisha threw himself a very unique going-away party. He slaughtered all his cattle and cooked their meat by burning all his farm equipment. He was symbolically and literally lighting fire to his exit strategy.

As he celebrated his new adventure with friends and family that night, they all knew he wouldn't be coming home, because he'd made sure he'd have nothing to come home to. He had removed the temptation. He had eliminated the exit strategy. His love for God moved him to make a dramatic commitment.

God honored Elisha's commitment. Elisha went on to become one of the most significant spiritual leaders in Israel's history. His love, faith, and commitment to God continue to inspire people around the globe.

KEEPING YOUR COMMITMENTS

Your life and your relationships will be defined by the commitments you make and how well you keep them.

Imagine how much richer and more vibrant your relationships could become if each one was built on a foundation of permanency. Love thrives where love is rooted in commitment. Make sure your loved ones know your love isn't just a fickle feeling; it's a promise for your shared future. Embrace a deeper sense of responsibility for and accountability to your loved ones, and you'll be cultivating fertile soil where lasting love can take root.

DISCUSSION QUESTIONS

1. What was the first commitment you remember making to someone?
2. How would relationships look different if people viewed love as a commitment rather than just a feeling?
3. Have you ever removed all exit strategies as Elisha did when he made his commitment to God?
4. What are some relationships in your life that would benefit from a stronger commitment?

CHAPTER 2

LOVE SELFLESSLY SACRIFICES

This is my commandment: Love each other in the same way I have loved you. There is no greater love than to lay down one's life for one's friends.

—JOHN 15:12–13

S he was afraid for her life. She was about to do the craziest thing imaginable, and love was to blame. She knew that the choice she was about to make had the potential to either change her life or possibly even end her life. Either way, she believed it had to be done.

This young woman was infamous in her town because of her profession. She was the subject of whispers, gossip, scorn, disgrace, and judgment. Many of her clients would gladly employ her services in the cover of darkness and then turn and point hypocritical, self-righteous fists in her direction in the daylight.

She had no place in society. She had no respect from her community, and she had no self-respect either. She felt she had no escape. She thought she deserved every harsh word and judgmental glare she had ever received. She believed this was simply who she was and all she could ever hope to be. She was a prostitute.

She had heard that Jesus would be visiting the home of a prominent religious leader in the community that day. She'd already heard Jesus' words and experienced his compassion. She was one of the many who had been changed by his love. He was perhaps the first man in her life who had looked at her with neither lust nor judgment in his eyes. Only love. He never touched her body, but he had been the first to touch her heart.

His love had broken her and invigorated her at the same time. She was a woman who had known the embrace of many men, but she had never known real love until she found Jesus, or rather, until Jesus found her. It was the purest and most powerful force she had ever experienced. His words made her see herself in a completely different light.

At first, she wasn't sure how to respond. All the confusion and past hurt left so many chaotic cracks in her heart that she struggled to believe she was even capable of giving or receiving love. Even still, she was drawn to Jesus with a force beyond anything she could explain. His love had given her things she'd never before received: healing for her past and hope for her future.

The tumultuous tug-of-war in her mind eventually led her to a crossroads between her old life of sin and a new life made possible by the love of Jesus. She knew that the decisions she made next about which path to pursue would define her present and her future. I'm sure she was tempted to retreat to familiar ground, which would have meant the comfortable misery of her old life. But for the first time, she dared to dream of a new life, and maybe even a new identity. Jesus' love had made it possible, and if she didn't respond to his love immediately, she feared she would regret it for eternity. Now was the time to act.

Before she could talk herself out of it, she found herself wandering into unfamiliar territory. She was an uninvited guest at a religious leader's home. Based on the customs and laws of the day, she could have been dragged out into the street and killed by stoning right then, but her love for Jesus was a stronger force than her instinct for self-preservation.

She made her way to Jesus as the party atmosphere of the room grew quiet at the scandalous scene unfolding before them. She knelt at the feet of Jesus, feet that would soon be nailed to a cross to pay the price for her sins, and ours as well, and she began to anoint them with expensive perfume. She had brought along her most valuable possession, perhaps her only valuable possession—an alabaster jar filled with perfume—and was now pouring it over the feet of her Savior.

The thick aroma quickly overwhelmed the room. The contents of the jar represented her old life. For her, the fragrance was the aroma of freedom. It was as if she were pouring out her very heart and soul.

The perfume was so valuable that it would have been a form of currency, a savings account, of sorts, of her earnings. It also represented her future in the seduction business, as a few drops of that fragrance would have made her more appealing to her potential clients on the streets.

None of that mattered now. She was pouring out her past, her present, and her future onto the feet of Jesus. In a scene of reckless abandon and uncontrolled emotion, she began to weep. As her tears mixed with the perfume, she kissed the feet of Jesus and dried them with her hair.

The host of the party, however, didn't see this as a beautiful act of love, but rather as an awkward interruption of his meal. The man began to mentally judge this woman and Jesus, as well, for allowing such a scene. Jesus, knowing the man's thoughts, took the opportunity to set the self-righteous host straight.

For all in the room to hear, and later recorded in the Bible for generations to read, Jesus applauded the young woman's act of love. His affirmation gave her the courage and strength she needed to move forward with her new life.

She experienced true peace, and it was all made possible because of the Prince of Peace. Jesus even proclaimed that for all time, wherever the good news of the Bible is taught, this woman's act of love would be remembered and discussed. True to Jesus' words, her example has been a model of love, courage, and faith that has inspired billions over the last two thousand years. Her inclusion in this book is just another footnote in her enduring legacy.

> ANYTIME WE LOVE SOMEONE, WE WILL EVENTUALLY BE COMPELLED TO MAKE A SELFLESS SACRIFICE.

Anytime we love someone, we will eventually be compelled to make a selfless sacrifice. Jesus didn't need this woman's perfume, but she needed to give it. The very act of the sacrifice became an important milestone in her journey.

Sometimes love will compel us to sacrifice because of a need in our own hearts, and other times we'll be called to sacrifice to meet a tangible need for the ones we love.

In some situations, the sacrifice will become an ongoing aspect of the relationship. We see this every day in people working to provide for their children, caring for aging parents, or even caring for their own spouses. Those selfless, sacrificial acts are a beautiful and powerful expression of love.

LOVE AND A GALLON OF MILK

My parents raised us in a home where they consistently modeled selfless love and self-sacrifice. Mom and Dad loved us, and their actions showed that there was nothing on earth they weren't willing to give up if it meant giving us something we needed. I've learned so much about love and faith from their beautiful example and ongoing influence in my life.

There was a time when I was around five years old when my family was very poor. The economy was terrible at the time, and my parents, like many parents, were struggling to make ends meet.

One day, Dad came home and found Mom crying. She is a very tenderhearted woman but she almost never cries, so Dad immediately knew something was wrong. He asked what the matter was, and through her tears she said, "There's no milk, and there's no money to buy more."

My parents, two of the hardest-working and most resourceful people on the planet, found themselves looking into the eyes of my crying baby brother and felt the desperation of not knowing how to provide for his most basic need. Dad started looking through the house for any spare change, but there was none to be found.

Then Dad had a thought and rushed into their bedroom. He opened his sock drawer and pulled out two shiny silver dollars. His great-grandmother had given them to him when he was a young boy. They were all he had left of her memory, but despite their great sentimental (and possibly even great financial) worth, in that moment their only value was their ability to meet a need for the people he loved.

Without hesitation, Dad walked to the store, grabbed a gallon of milk, and slapped those two silver dollars on the counter.

That's what love looks like.

I told that story in a sermon at church recently, and my parents happened to be sitting in the crowd. I got to the end and found myself gripped by emotion as I reflected on the lifetime of love and support I've received from them both. I looked down and saw that they were crying, too, and I told them I love them.

When I looked back up, everyone else was also crying. Most people look really ugly when they cry. I certainly do. My face contorts to a likeness of Sloth from the movie *The Goonies*. Even so, this undoubtedly was a beautiful moment.

It's funny to think that a two-dollar purchase of milk could cause a ripple effect that inspired people three decades later, but that's how love works. Those sacrifices we make, both big and small, make a lasting impact. The milk may expire quickly, but the love lasts forever.

LOVE AND A DIAMOND RING

When we truly love someone, the sacrifices we make feel much more like a privilege than an obligation.

I remember the feelings of joy and anticipation when I was ready to purchase an engagement ring for Ashley. I was a college student, and I was poor in a way that only college students can understand. I was broke, but I was in love, and love always finds a way.

Ashley understood my lack of resources and would have happily married me without an engagement ring, but I wanted to give one to her. I realized that this simple piece of jewelry wasn't just a culturally enforced tradition perpetuated by greedy jewelers; it was an opportunity to express my love and commitment to my future bride in a way that would bring a huge smile to her face. I knew it would also create a tangible reminder of this season of our journey together. In addition to that, it would get me in the habit of self-sacrifice for the sake of my bride, which is a vital habit for any healthy marriage.

After doing some research on the cut and clarity of diamonds, I felt ready to go shopping. It wasn't long before I was in the mall jewelry store holding the perfect ring. The only problem was that I didn't have any money. Luckily, they had a layaway program where I could have ninety days to make payments on it, and when the last payment was made, I could come by the store and pick it up.

They say, "A diamond is forever." I'm not sure if that's true, but for a long time, I thought the payments would last forever!

Ninety days sounded like a lot of time to my young mind, but a few days in, I hadn't made any money and I started calculating how much income I'd need to average per day to pay off the ring in time. I knew I needed to take quick action, so I started applying for jobs anywhere I could. The minimum wage I'd been making on campus as part of the landscaping crew wasn't going to cut it, so I looked for server jobs or sales jobs or anything that might produce more income.

Though it's not my nature to walk into a place and ask for a job, love had made me fearless. I boldly walked up to one potential employer after another with my résumé in hand, but over and over the answer was no.

I was discouraged but undaunted. I finally landed what I thought would be a perfect job as a server for a high-end hotel restaurant, but I rushed my way through the personality profile thinking it was only a formality. It turns out the personality profile was more than a formality, and I actually failed it.

I didn't think it was even possible to fail a personality profile, but somehow I did. That's right. You're reading a book written by a guy who couldn't pass a test that many convicted felons working at the same place had easily passed. It was not my proudest moment. My friend Smitty later went to work at that place, and for years afterward, he would introduce me to his coworkers as "the guy who failed the personality profile."

From what I can tell, I became something of an urban legend at the restaurant as the only guy who had ever failed the test. I didn't dwell on the blow to my pride for too long, though, because I didn't have time. There were only eighty-three days left to pay off this ring, and I had to quickly figure out a way to do it.

I weighed my options and pulled out my phone to call up an old friend who managed an electronics store. I wasn't any good with electronics. In fact, I barely knew how to operate my cell phone (and this was back before the phones were even smart).

I opted not to tell him that I was electronically illiterate and that I had just flunked a personality profile. I figured I could get past my technology deficiencies by working hard and leaning heavily on my people skills to make up the difference. I explained that I was highly motivated because I had a limited window of time to pay for a ring for a girl who was way out of my league and I wanted to seal the deal as fast as I could. My friend graciously agreed to give me a shot, and I was on the job the next day.

The learning curve at the new job was even steeper than I had anticipated, but my resolve had never been stronger. I studied harder than I'd studied for any class I'd ever taken in school. I wasn't just working for a good grade; I was working for my future bride.

I was picturing the smile on her face when I put that ring on her finger. I was imagining her saying, "Yes!" and jumping into my arms. I was picturing the scene of telling our future children and grandchildren the story of how I'd proposed and what her response had been. I was working for much more than just a diamond. I was working for the opportunity to create a timeless moment, a moment that would lead to a lifelong journey with the one I loved.

After hundreds of hours, scores of cell-phone sales, dozens of training manuals, and a lot of hard work, I finally had enough money to pay off the ring. On day eighty-eight of the ninety-day layaway, I proudly marched to the cashier of the jewelry store and made my final payment. I ransomed that beautiful little ring and held it in my hands like I'd just climbed on a podium to receive an Olympic gold medal!

It was my prized possession, and I couldn't wait to give it away. That's the beautiful irony of love. The only way we can truly keep it is to give it away. The moment I placed that ring on her finger and saw the look on her face, every minute of the work and worry seemed well worth the effort.

THE ULTIMATE SACRIFICE

Most of us are willing to make reasonable sacrifices for the ones we love. We'd spend our last two dollars to buy milk for our children. We'd work overtime to purchase an engagement ring for a future bride. Those sacrifices cost us something, but they don't cost us everything.

The ultimate test of love comes when a person is asked to give up all they value for the sake of another. We see this type of selfless heroism on battlefields when one soldier jumps on a live grenade to absorb the explosion and save the lives of his fellow soldiers. Jesus taught that there is no greater love than to willingly lay down your own life for the sake of others.

> THE ULTIMATE TEST OF LOVE COMES WHEN A PERSON IS ASKED TO GIVE UP ALL THEY VALUE FOR THE SAKE OF ANOTHER.

First Lieutenant Alonzo Cushing was a twenty-two-year-old officer in the Union army during the Civil War when he made the ultimate sacrifice. The young West Point graduate was in charge of six cannons and more than one hundred men during the Battle of Gettysburg. His small force found itself trapped in the middle of the battlefield during the Confederate army's infamous assault known as Pickett's Charge.

The full force of the rebels was closing in on Cushing and his men. The young officer had already been shot twice and was critically wounded. He had every right to retreat to safety, but he recognized the magnitude of the moment. Instead, he ordered the cannons moved to the front lines, and he limped forward to lead a counterattack. His courage and tenacity inspired the men around him, and they fought back valiantly before Cushing was shot again. The final shot proved to be fatal.

The sacrifice of one young man turned the tide of a battle, which turned the tide of a war, which ultimately held a nation together. His love for his country prompted him to sacrifice his life in honorable service. He didn't live to see the impact of his sacrifice, but the world was changed because of his courage.

Alonzo Cushing was posthumously awarded the Congressional Medal of Honor in the year 2014. It's the military's highest honor for service and bravery above and beyond the call of duty. The recognition came more than a century and a half after his death.

Sometimes you'll live to see the impact of your sacrifices, and sometimes you won't. We don't make our sacrifices for recognition; we make our sacrifices for

> SOMETIMES YOU'LL LIVE TO SEE THE IMPACT OF YOUR SACRIFICES, AND SOMETIMES YOU WON'T. WE DON'T MAKE OUR SACRIFICES FOR RECOGNITION; WE MAKE OUR SACRIFICES FOR LOVE.

love. When love moves you to sacrifice, you can rest assured that lives will be changed and eternity will be impacted.

THE ULTIMATE TEST

When I think about the ultimate test of love, my mind goes back to a story I first learned in Sunday school when I was a small child. This test of love and faith made a profound impression on my young mind.

Abraham was an old man enjoying the twilight years with his wife, Sarah. They had been unable to have children, and due to their advanced ages, the dream for a family had died many decades earlier.

Now God was promising Abraham and Sarah that they would have a child. Sarah laughed out loud at the idea. On the surface, it did seem pretty ridiculous. She was probably thinking,

I'm going to be the only person at Walmart buying diapers for my baby and diapers for my husband and me at the same time!

God has a great sense of humor. Since he invented laughter, I suppose we shouldn't be surprised that he also creates plenty of scenarios that induce laughter. True to his promise, God gave Abraham and Sarah a son. The only logical name for the boy was Isaac, because the name literally means "laughter."

Isaac was the apple of Abraham's eye. He was the tangible proof of God's faithfulness. He embodied the promise of the great nation God would birth through Abraham's lineage. He was the first in a line of descendants who would someday rival the stars in the sky in number.

Isaac was Abraham's whole life. For that reason, Isaac became the perfect test. God told Abraham to take Isaac up the mountain where he was to build an altar and sacrifice his son. Abraham was commanded to kill Isaac.

On the surface, this test may seem barbaric and cruel, but once you see how it plays out, you'll probably have a different perspective. Obedience to God's commands always brings blessings not only to ourselves but also for the glory of God. This situation would prove to be no different.

As you can imagine, Abraham was heartbroken at even the thought of carrying out this task. He loved his son more than life. I'm sure his head was spinning in a thousand different directions as he tried to make sense of this seemingly incomprehensible mission given from a loving God.

Abraham finally came to the place where he decided faith doesn't mean having everything figured out. Faith is a choice, not a feeling. Faith means choosing to trust God even when life doesn't seem to make sense.

Abraham told Isaac that they needed to load up their donkey

and make a trip up the mountain to give a sacrifice to God. In their era, it wasn't uncommon to make burnt offerings to God with slaughtered animals, but in this case, they were making the trip up the mountain without a suitable animal. Isaac kept asking his father about this logistical oversight, and Abraham would answer cryptically, "My son, the Lord Himself will provide the sacrifice."

They made it up the mountain, and once the altar was built, Abraham picked up his young son and placed him on it. I've often wondered what was going through Abraham's and Isaac's minds in this defining moment. I'm sure both their lives flashed before their eyes as Abraham raised the knife. What happened next was extraordinary. I want you to hear this next part straight from the source:

> At that moment the angel of the LORD called to him from heaven, "Abraham! Abraham!"
>
> "Yes," Abraham replied. "Here I am!"
>
> "Don't lay a hand on the boy!" the angel said. "Do not hurt him in any way, for now I know that you truly fear God. You have not withheld from me even your son, your only son" (Gen. 22:11–12).

It had all been a test. Abraham had shown he was willing to make the ultimate sacrifice out of love and obedience to God. The test, however, wasn't only for Abraham. It was masterfully written into God's unfolding story of grace to foreshadow the greatest act of love the world would ever know.

Centuries later, God would make the ultimate sacrifice on our behalf. He would place his only son on an altar. The altar would be in the shape of a cross.

Isaac was rescued at the last moment, but Jesus was not. Jesus could have called down an army of angels to rescue him, but love compelled him to stay. The father and the son followed through on the ultimate sacrifice motivated by love for you and for me. God never intended for Abraham to sacrifice his son, but it was a price that God himself was prepared to pay to ransom humanity from the penalty of sin.

> JESUS COULD HAVE CALLED DOWN AN ARMY OF ANGELS TO RESCUE HIM, BUT LOVE COMPELLED HIM TO STAY.

GOD'S SACRIFICE FOR YOU

I don't know your story, but God does. Maybe you've been burned by love. Perhaps you've had people express their love to you with words, but those words turned out to be empty with no actions to follow them up. Maybe the hardships of life and failed relationships have caused you to think that God must not care about you.

If you get nothing else out of this entire book, I want you to get this: *God loves you.*

He doesn't love you with some impersonal kind of love, like you're rolled up into some nameless, faceless mob with the other seven billion people on earth. No, he loves you with a deeply personal kind of love. He knit you together in your mother's womb, and even then, he loved you more than you can imagine. God is an infinite God, and he loves you infinitely more than you can comprehend.

When Jesus hung on that cross in torturous pain, his love for you kept him there. Sure, he was giving his life for the entirety of the human race, but it was also for you, personally. You never need to doubt the fact that you are loved; Jesus' sacrifice for you on the cross is evidence enough.

It will give you strength and courage to sacrifice for those you love. No matter how much you give, you'll never be able to outgive what has already been given for you. Remember, when love compels you to make a selfless sacrifice, it will cost you something, but what you gain in the process is always more valuable than what you give away.

EMBRACING GOD'S SACRIFICE FOR YOU

The Academy Award-winning World War II movie *Saving Private Ryan* tells the story of a young soldier (Private Ryan) whose brothers have been killed in battle. To spare his family the agony of losing all of their sons, the government orchestrates a rescue mission to save him and send him home. The rescue team is led by a no-nonsense army captain who seems to believe that the whole thing is a bad idea.

In the film's final scene, the captain is fatally wounded while fulfilling his mission. With his dying words, he looks the soldier in the eyes and says, "Earn this! Earn it." The film flashes forward many decades, and we see Private Ryan as an old man standing at the grave of that captain. You can tell he has been haunted by those words and trying to "earn it" all his life, but he never knows for sure if he has measured up. He pleads with the grave, seeking approval, but he finds none.

Many people believe they have put their faith in Jesus, but they also believe they have to earn what he did for them on the cross. Here's the good news: when Jesus was hanging on that cross, dying to save you, he did not use his dying words to say, "Earn this." Do you know what he said instead? He said, "It is finished!"

Did you catch that? It is finished. That means done, complete, sealed, finished! That's God's gift of grace. Jesus has done *all* the work already. You couldn't possibly earn it even if you tried with everything you had, and God never expected you to.

The Bible says that if you confess that Jesus is Lord and believe in your heart that God raised him from the dead, then you will be saved (Rom. 10:9). It's not a duty for you to earn; it's a gift for you to receive by faith. Reach out to your Savior and love God with your whole heart, mind, soul, and strength. He's already done all the work, and he did it out of love for you. It is finished.

DISCUSSION QUESTIONS

1. Has there ever been a time in your life when someone selflessly sacrificed for you? How did that sacrifice change your view of love?
2. What's the greatest sacrifice you've made for someone you love?
3. How would your relationships look different if there were mutual selflessness from all people involved?
4. Do you believe it's possible to sacrifice too much for the ones you love? Why or why not?

CHAPTER 3

LOVE SPEAKS TRUTH

We will speak the truth in love, growing in every way more and more like Christ.

—EPHESIANS 4:15

One of the core values in the Willis household is honesty. Our kids know that they can get in trouble for lots of things, but lying tops the list of deadly sins. We put so much value on honesty because we want our kids to realize that love is built on trust. So if we want to keep our family strong, we've always got to tell one another the truth.

We went through several years when the kids learned this tell-the-truth lesson so well that it nearly backfired on us. They assumed that because the truth was so important, if they considered something to be true, they could say it out loud. On the surface, this doesn't seem like a bad thing until we had some very embarrassing interactions in public.

Here are a few examples from the long list of unfiltered "truths" that my children spoke to strangers in public:

"Wow, you have a huge belly!"

"You look really old like Yoda."

"You smell funny."

"Why are you dressed like that? Are you poor?"

"Are you going to feed milk to the baby from your nipples?"

That last one actually referred to me. Apparently, I have "man boobs."

As you can imagine, we preferred to keep these kinds of phrases from being blurted out in public to complete strangers. My first thought was, *Let's just stop taking the kids to Walmart!* For some reason, a lot of these incidents seemed to happen at Walmart. Kids seem to behave better when we're at Target.

We knew that isolating the kids in solitary confinement until adulthood wouldn't work, so we needed a new strategy that kept the emphasis on truth but also put a filter in the process. Our friends the Asselin family had a policy that worked great, so we stole theirs.

They taught their kids that they weren't allowed to say anything to anyone unless it met three criteria:

1. It had to be true.
2. It had to be kind.
3. It had to be necessary.

TKN: True, Kind, and Necessary.

This became a mantra of ours as well. We told our kids that truth was vital, but the truth alone wasn't enough. You could say something that was technically right, but if you said it without love and compassion, you were still wrong.

We quickly got some real-world testing grounds to try the new policy. We were at the grocery store, and the boys were hovering around the cart looking for candy to sneak in while I wasn't looking. An elderly lady limped past on her cane, and I held my breath as the boys started to say something. They quickly caught themselves and bit their tongues. Then, while she was still just a few steps away, they shouted with pride, "Dad! We did it! That really old lady just walked by, and we didn't even tell her that she looked old like Yoda!"

I patted the boys on the head while giving an awkward smile to the sweet lady who heard every word of their commentary. Like most life lessons, this was a work in progress, but I'm happy to report that the boys are getting better with it every day.

WOUNDS FROM A FRIEND

Speaking the truth in love doesn't mean you should never communicate a painful truth to someone. In fact, the Bible teaches that painful truths from a friend can be trusted, but an enemy just tells you what you want to hear. A mark of true friendship and real love is a commitment to be the one to speak a painful truth.

Sometimes this will be seen in little things, such as a friend or relative being willing to tell you your fly is unzipped or you have something stuck in your teeth. A mere acquaintance or enemy would just walk away giggling and let you figure it out on your own.

This principle also holds true in bigger issues. If you're in an unhealthy relationship or you've developed some dangerous or self-destructive habits, loved ones will have the courage to intervene. They'll refuse to just tell you what you want to hear.

Even if you hate them for saying it, they'll say it because they love you.

THE TRUTH ISN'T ALWAYS COMFORTABLE, BUT IT'S ALWAYS NECESSARY.

Think back over your life. Have there ever been times you've had someone express a deep and sincere concern for you by pointing out a painful truth? That's the mark of a real friend. The truth isn't always comfortable, but it's always necessary.

THE TRUTH WILL SET YOU FREE

Jesus famously told us in Scripture that the truth has the power to set us free, and his statement has been quoted in courtrooms, movies, and countless other places ever since. It's a beautiful thought, but it's also a powerful truth. When we find the courage to confess our secrets, there is nothing to hinder our lives or our love.

I've watched this principle hold true countless times within the relational dynamic of marriage. Trust is vital in any healthy relationship, but the stakes are highest within the context of marriage. Marriage was created by God to be a relationship of complete unity and transparency, so deception of any kind will undermine the foundation of the marriage covenant. I tell couples often, "Your marriage will never be stronger than your trust in each other."

If a married couple can't trust each other, they can't fully function. A husband and wife must operate like two wings on the same bird; if they don't work together in full partnership, the marriage will never get off the ground. Trust makes that possible. When we replace trust with secrecy, we're erecting invisible barriers to limit the growth in our marriages. Secrecy is the enemy of intimacy.

I recently met with a woman from our church who had been having an extramarital affair. She was disgusted by her actions, but she was also very apprehensive about confessing them to her husband. In her mind, the secret would protect him from pain, and she could handle it on her own. The reality of trying to keep that secret caused all kinds of strife in her relationship, because with every interaction and every question from him about what was bothering her, she would have to perpetuate a lie in order to keep the status quo.

Jesus famously said, "And you will know the truth, and the truth will set you free" (John 8:32). Those words are carved in the marble of courthouses and academic halls all over the world, but this statement is also a powerful principle for healthy relationships. Honesty always paves the way to intimacy.

I reminded her that Jesus knew what he was talking about, and the truth really does have the power to set us free. She agreed, and we prayed that she would have the strength to confess and to work to rebuild trust. We also prayed that her husband would have the grace to give healing a chance.

She went home and told her husband, and his response shocked her. As you can imagine, he was heartbroken, but he was also relieved. Through his tears, he said that he knew something was terribly wrong, but the uncertainty and the secrecy in their marriage had been tearing him apart. He was thankful to finally know the truth. Now that the root issue was out in the open, they could work together to address it.

When a problem is hidden, there's nothing you can do to fix it. Once it's out in the open, the healing process can finally begin.

That single conversation began a brand-new chapter for this couple. They both opened up with a level of honesty and vulnerability that had been absent. Through a

A PAINFUL TRUTH IS ALWAYS BETTER THAN A HIDDEN LIE.

long period of healing, counseling, and personal growth, this couple is now much happier and healthier than they've ever been. It wasn't an easy journey, but they'd be the first to tell you to get your secrets out in the open. A painful truth is always better than a hidden lie.

WHEN THE TRUTH COSTS

One of the biggest temptations in parenting is to practice selective honesty in front of our children. I was faced with this temptation a few weeks ago when my family went to an amusement park. We had already paid a lot of money just to park in the parking lot, and now we were about to pay the inflated ticket prices at the park entrance.

I was studying the sign and saw that children under age three were free. Our son Chandler had just turned three years old days before. He's small for his age and looks younger than three. The cashier looked at our kids and asked the question: "How old are the kids?"

I wanted to say, "Actually, all of them are toddlers. The big ones are just mutants who look exceptionally old, but they're all under three years old. Two adult tickets, please."

I knew that approach probably wouldn't work, but I was completely confident I could get at least Chandler in for free. He just missed the cutoff by a few days, and nobody would know the difference. Besides, the park was already getting plenty of our money, so they wouldn't need the extra cash.

I was having this argument in my mind and trying to justify telling a lie to save a little money, but then I looked at my kids and asked myself, *What lesson do I want to teach them? Can I expect them to be honest with me about everything when I'm not willing to do the same? Do I really want to teach them that telling the truth is important, but it's not as important as saving a little money?*

Selective honesty is the same as dishonesty. I quickly came to my senses and paid the exorbitant ticket price, because the price of the ticket was much less expensive than what I would have given up in terms of my integrity and credibility with my kids. The truth might be expensive at times, but it's always worth it.

> THE TRUTH MIGHT BE EXPENSIVE AT TIMES, BUT IT'S ALWAYS WORTH IT.

A dramatic example of this can be learned from a local hero named Bobby Jones. If you are a golf fan, you already know the name. He was considered the greatest golfer of his generation, and he eventually cofounded the Augusta National Golf Course and the Masters Golf Tournament, which is widely regarded as the greatest annual event in all of global sports. Living near Augusta, I get to enjoy the living legacy of this golf legend. You can't get anywhere in this town without turning onto a road named after him.

His legacy has been so enduring because it's built on more than just his skill. The world is full of skilled athletes whose names we'll never remember. Jones, however, was fueled by a pure love for the sport. He passed up a fortune in earnings because he refused to accept any prize money for playing. He felt that being paid to play cheapened the game. He also established trust by being willing to tell the truth even when it hurt.

The most dramatic example of his honesty came during the 1925 US Open. He was leading by one stroke when he moved his club to get set up for his next shot, and the ball moved slightly due to inadvertent contact. Nobody saw the ball move. There were no television cameras. The movement had been so slight that his own caddie hadn't noticed it. Nobody but Bobby Jones saw the movement, but Jones immediately knew what had to be done.

He marched over to the official and declared that he needed to call a foul on himself. He explained the infraction, but nobody seemed excited to enforce it. After all, it was so minor that there was no evidence a foul had actually occurred. Jones persisted because he knew that compromising would be a blow to his personal integrity and a blow to the integrity of the game he loved. He insisted that the rules be followed and a one-stroke penalty be issued.

The tournament continued, and Bobby Jones ultimately lost the US Open by one stroke. He still preferred an honest second-place performance to a trophy won by deception.

You might put yourself in that situation and think of all kinds of reasons to justify not telling the truth. There are many. Jones could have easily kept quiet, but even if nobody else ever knew, he would always know the truth. And he wasn't willing to live a lie. When we give a tiny foothold to justified deceit in our minds, it quickly opens the door to destruction.

Bobby Jones's honesty, humility, passion, and skill transcended the sport of golf and inspired people from all walks of life. This single example of honesty is still retold today to give encouragement and instruction in the importance of truth. That's a legacy much more significant than any golf trophy.

BE HONEST WITH YOURSELF

We all tend to craft a self-focused view of the world where we emerge as either a hero or a victim in every scene. We're never the villains in the story. The truth is, though, that we've all been the bad guy more often than we'd like to admit. A life of love requires that we look in the mirror and give an honest and humble self-assessment.

> A LIFE OF LOVE REQUIRES THAT WE LOOK IN THE MIRROR AND GIVE AN HONEST AND HUMBLE SELF-ASSESSMENT.

Jesus once made an analogy that we as human beings seem to be experts at noticing a speck of sawdust in somebody else's eye, but we'll completely ignore the wooden plank sticking out of our own eyes. We can be so quick to see the flaws in others and so blind to the obvious flaws in ourselves.

We tend to create this kind of hierarchy of sin where our sins aren't nearly as bad as somebody else's. We become experts at pointing our fingers at the guys who are "worse" than we are, which makes us feel justified in our sins.

Say, for instance, you fudge the numbers on your taxes. You might say, "It's no big deal! The government doesn't need that money. They'd just blow it. I worked hard for this. Maybe it's technically wrong, but there are worse things I could be doing on my computer than creative accounting on my taxes. The guy who shares my cubicle at work, he looks at porn on his computer! That's worse than what I do, right?"

And the guy who looks at pornography might say, "So what? I look at porn. I'm a grown man, and I can do what I want. It's not hurting anybody. It's just fantasy. I'm not like my boss. He's actually cheating on his wife. What I'm doing isn't as bad as an actual affair, right?"

And the boss might say, "So I'm having an affair. I'm not proud of it, but I'm just a man. It's not even against the law. I could be doing much worse things. Like the guy we fired for stealing. He got arrested. He's in prison for embezzlement. That's way worse than what I'm doing, right?"

And the thief might say, "So I took some money, but I never hurt anybody. My cell mate has killed a guy! That's way worse than what I did, right?"

> GOD WANTS US TO HAVE A HEART FOR LOVING UNLOVABLE PEOPLE BECAUSE THAT'S WHAT GOD DID FOR US.

And the cell mate might say, "Okay, you got me. I killed a guy, but it was only one guy and he wasn't even nice! I'm nothing like the guy on death row down the hall. He's a serial killer! He's killed lots of people! That's way worse than me, right?"

And the serial killer might respond, "So I'm a serial killer. Nobody's perfect. But don't be too quick to judge me, because I never once cheated on my taxes!"

You get the idea. Until we can look in the mirror and come to terms with our own sins and our own desperate need for God's grace, we'll never be able to see ourselves or others through the lens of love. God wants us to have a heart for loving unlovable people because that's what God did for us. He loved us much more than we could ever deserve, and he calls us to do the same for others.

YOUR LEGACY OF TRUTH

What kind of legacy do you want for your own life? What stories do you want people telling about you a generation after your death? The decisions you are making right now are shaping future generations. Your legacy will be measured by your relationships, and your relationships will only be as strong as the trust your loved ones have in you.

DISCUSSION QUESTIONS

1. Do you remember a time when you had to speak a difficult truth to someone you love? How did he or she respond?
2. Do you remember a time when someone you love spoke a difficult truth to you? How did you respond?
3. Have you ever had a relationship with a lack of trust for the other person? What complications did the distrust create?
4. How would your relationships look different if there were complete trust at all times?

CHAPTER 4

LOVE CONQUERS FEAR

There is no fear in love. But perfect love drives out fear.

—1 JOHN 4:18 NIV

When Ashley and I were newlyweds, we had just settled comfortably into our little house in Georgetown, Kentucky, next to the college campus where I had graduated a week before our wedding. The Love Shack, as we called it, was already starting to feel like home, but the age of the house combined with some cracks in the foundation made it possible for critters to find their way inside.

This was a problem for me, because for some weird reason I've always been freaked out by mice. I even struggle going to Disney World because I'm afraid Mickey is going to start chasing me! It's actually not quite that bad, but it's still a pretty embarrassing fear. At this point in our young marriage, I had done a pretty good job of hiding my fears and frailties from my bride, but she was about to learn in dramatic fashion that her husband wasn't nearly as tough as he pretended to be.

She was doing crunches on the floor in front of the TV while I was doing no physical movement at all lounging in a recliner. Out of the corner of my eye, I saw a quick movement, and I turned my head to see two beady little eyes staring back at me. My fear was staring me in the face.

I gathered my wits and summoned my courage. I was going to take care of this mouse. I refused to be bullied by a rodent in my home in front of my wife. After all, I was the man of the house, and I was about to teach this mouse a lesson. This was a moment of destiny!

I tiptoed to the kitchen and found a large pot and started moving toward the mouse. In hindsight, I'm not entirely sure what I was planning to do with the pot. I think I was planning to capture the mouse under the pot, and then I was hoping Ashley would know what to do from there.

As I took a step toward Mickey, he saw me and made his move. I remember thinking to myself that mice are much faster than you'd think. He started running toward Ashley, who was still on the floor doing sit-ups, but he didn't see her because he was looking back toward me as he ran. Before I could say anything to warn her, the mouse had run into Ashley's side and scurried his little mouse feet up onto her stomach.

At this point, all chaos broke loose. There was literally shrieking, screaming, and crying. It was a full-blown, hysterical meltdown. Finally, Ashley had to say, "Dave, pull yourself together! It is just a mouse!"

She's still the brave one in the relationship.

We survived the mouse attack and we've laughed about it a lot since then, but that incident also taught us a valuable lesson. Many of the things that cause us worry and stress are no more threatening or dangerous than that mouse, but we let them rob us of our peace or distract us from the issues that really are worth our attention.

UNLEARNING YOUR FEARS

Many people live a life led by fear instead of being led by love. Fear can be the reason why a relationship ends or the reason why a relationship never begins in the first place. Our fears can cloud our judgment and erode the trust, intimacy, and peace of mind in a relationship. Fear may be something natural, but love represents something supernatural. Love has the power to set a positive course for your life and chase away your fears in the process.

FEAR MAY BE SOMETHING NATURAL, BUT LOVE REPRESENTS SOMETHING SUPERNATURAL.

I believe we all have fears; and those fears, if left unchecked, can rob our relationships and our lives of peace and joy. Some of those fears might be relatively harmless (like my very unmanly mouse phobia), but some come from places of very deep pain. Perhaps you had a parent walk out on your family, and over time that emotional wound and feeling of rejection created a fear of abandonment. Maybe you survived a near-drowning in childhood, and now you still break out into a cold sweat every time you're near the water.

The first step in overcoming is to understand the root. All of our fears are learned. The only innate fears you had at birth were a prewired fear of loud noises and a fear of falling. Those are the only stimuli that create a fear response from an infant. I'm assuming you've overcome those fears; so every fear you've got now is something you've learned along the way. And since you learned it, you can also unlearn it.

To start identifying the root of some of your fears, I want you to pick one thing that causes fear, worry, or anxiety when you think of it. Now, I want you to think back to your earliest memory of feeling that same fear. Was there a single incident that put the fear into motion? Was there a series of incidents causing a chain reaction?

When we're in our young and formational years, it's kind of like we have wet cement in our minds and hearts. I don't know if you've ever carved your initials into the wet cement on a sidewalk, but they dry quickly and can last for a very long time. The impressions left in your mind and heart from childhood harden over time, and those impressions, whether positive and loving or negative and harmful, create lasting marks that can shape our worldviews and our approaches to life and love.

MAKING PEACE WITH THE PAST

One of the most important ways to break free from your present fears is to make peace with your past hurts.

When I was a kid, one of my favorite movies was *Back to the Future*. I was fascinated by the idea of traveling through time and changing history. I even spotted an old DeLorean in our neighborhood and was tempted to peek inside to see if Doc and Marty McFly were lost in time and looking for a way back to 1985. (I'm kind of a dork when it comes to my fascination with 1980s movies.)

As much as I love those movies, what I've found as I've gotten older is that traveling to the past makes for good entertainment but a very poor way to live in real life. We do have the power to shape the future, but unless you actually own a time machine, worrying about the past is a complete waste of your time and energy. If you want to live a life of love and the freedom it brings, you've got to make peace with your past.

> IF YOU WANT TO LIVE A LIFE OF LOVE AND THE FREEDOM IT BRINGS, YOU'VE GOT TO MAKE PEACE WITH YOUR PAST.

We should learn from our past and build on our past but not ever dwell on our past. Just like the rearview mirror in your car, looking at the past gives us perspective; but if you're staring at it all the time, you're going to cause a wreck. We need to embrace the moment we are in. Don't let regrets from yesterday or worries about tomorrow rob you of the peace and blessings God has for you today!

If you are one of the many who feels stuck in a rut of living in past regrets or trying to recreate past glories, here are a few principles to help you move forward:

1. Your past sins were all paid for on the cross.

Jesus took the punishment that was meant for you and me, and by faith in him, we are totally forgiven. From the cross he said, "It is finished!" He didn't say, "You'd better spend the rest of your life feeling bad about what you did." He came to give you life and freedom, so don't beat yourself up for mistakes that he has literally already taken the beating for. It's time to let go.

2. Your past does not define you.

It's easy to believe the lie that the things we have done and the things that have been done to us are what give us our identities. The truth is that your past has helped shape your character, but it has nothing to do with your identity. Your identity comes from God alone, and he loves you unconditionally.

3. Your best days are ahead.

Don't get trapped trying to recreate the good old days when your best days are still to come. Celebrate warm memories and milestones, but don't live your life in an artificial time warp. Each day God has new blessings in store for you. Every sunrise is a reminder that our God is always creating new beginnings and new opportunities. Don't miss them by looking back.

The song that set the tone for the whole *Back to the Future* soundtrack was "The Power of Love." If there was a movie about your life, I'm convinced God would want "The Power of Love" to set the tone. It might not be the actual song (although Huey Lewis rocks) but God makes possible the power to bring peace to your past, freedom to your present, and hope for your future.

MOVING FROM PAST FEARS TO PRESENT FEARS

There isn't enough room in your heart for both fear and faith, so each day you must decide which one gets to stay.

Our fears are much broader than the "big" fears like death or tragedy. Some of the most insidious fears are the seemingly insignificant ones that can rob us of peace on a daily basis. One of the most intimidating daily fears in my life is facing the morning chaos of getting our boys ready for school. That might sound like a ridiculous fear, but I'm serious. It feels like every morning becomes a frantic race against time as we loudly and clumsily try to get to school before the tardy bell.

One morning, I was getting our boys ready for school, which is a massive undertaking and makes me respect my wife even more, because she is normally the one doing it. Amid the screaming infant and two complaining grade-schoolers, there was a mess in the kitchen, a dirty diaper on the floor, toothpaste on the sink, and stress in the air. When we finally got out the door, one of the boys had forgotten something and had to run back in. The door was open just long enough for (I'm not making this up) a bird to fly in the house.

After I eventually got the bird out (unharmed) and the kids loaded, just before I pulled out onto the main road a garbage truck cut me off and started driving about five miles per hour and stopping at every other house. I wasn't sure whether to scream or laugh at the irony of it.

In the grand scheme of things, a stressful morning doesn't impact life or eternity all that much. But in those longer seasons of joblessness, sickness, financial stress, marriage strain, and other ongoing life events, the frustration and fear can seem overwhelming. Here are a few things I've learned to remember that have helped me in those challenging seasons of life.

These principles have been an ongoing source of courage and perspective for me, and I pray they help you as well.

1. Remember that your character should always be stronger than your circumstances.

We can't always control what happens to us, but we can always control how we choose to respond. In those moments when I choose to stop complaining and instead to give thanks to God for the good in my life, the parts that seem bad start to seem much less significant. Choose to keep a positive attitude and a thankful heart regardless of what you're going through.

> And let the peace that comes from Christ rule in your hearts. For as members of one body you are called to live in peace. And always be thankful (Col. 3:15).

2. Remember that your struggles always lead to strength.

Every difficulty in your life, whether big or small, is something God will use to produce more strength, faith, and perseverance in you if you let him. All your pain has a purpose.

> And have you forgotten the encouraging words God spoke to you as his children? He said, "My child, don't make light of the LORD's discipline, and don't give up when he corrects you. For the LORD disciplines those he loves, and he punishes each one he accepts as his child" (Heb. 12:5–6).

3. Remember that God's timing is always perfect.

God's plans are almost always different from our plans, but his plans are always perfect. Have the patience to wait on his timing instead of forcing your own.

> Better to be patient than powerful; better to have self-control than to conquer a city (Prov. 16:32).

4. Remember that God will never leave your side.

You may feel like you're going through this struggle all alone, but from the moment you ask Jesus to bring you into

God's family, he will be by your side to the end. So never lose hope.

> Don't be afraid, for I am with you. Don't be discouraged, for I am your God. I will strengthen you and help you. I will hold you up with my victorious right hand (Isa. 41:10).

50,000 VOLTS OF FEAR

Courage isn't the absence of fear; it's the presence of love in the face of fear. Maybe you're in a season of your life when you're going through something difficult. Fear seems to be creeping in from all sides, and you're asking yourself, *If God is so loving and so powerful, then why am I going through all this pain in the first place?*

That's a great question, and I certainly don't want to minimize your pain with any kind of clichéd answer, but a friend of mine shared a story with me recently that has helped shape my answer to the question of why God allows pain in the world.

COURAGE ISN'T THE ABSENCE OF FEAR; IT'S THE PRESENCE OF LOVE IN THE FACE OF FEAR.

My friend Billy is one of the toughest guys I know. He is a police officer in Georgia, where I live, and when he tells me about his days, it makes my days seem painfully boring in comparison. Whenever we meet up, he'll ask me what I did, and I'll typically say, "I had a few meetings, wrote a blog post, met up with a guy for some coffee. What did you do?"

"Me? I went in with the SWAT team to take out a drug

kingpin, got into a fistfight with a guy trying to carjack somebody, and found ten pounds of marijuana hidden in a guy's trunk."

He wins the "What did you do today?" game every time.

On the day of this story, Billy had to go to a training session to be allowed to carry a Taser. They are powerful crime-suppressing tools, because nobody wants to get shot with 50,000 volts of electricity! Billy knew that carrying this tool would potentially save his life and the lives of others, but to be certified to carry a Taser, you have to allow yourself to be shot by one. It was one of the first days ever that my job seemed cooler than his. As a pastor, I've had to go through a lot, but I've never once been electrocuted.

For months, my fearless friend was sweating bullets and dreading the day he would have to "ride the lightning." The day finally came, and after a brief instructional meeting, Billy was led into an ominous room where two large men stood on either side of him to hold him up while the electricity coursed through his body.

He sheepishly walked toward his doom, and as the beefy dudes on each side of him held him up, one asked him if he was ready. Before he could even answer the question, he felt two sharp metal prongs shoot into his back, followed by eight seconds of the most excruciating pain he had ever experienced. It was worse than he even imagined, but it also ended quickly.

Billy was able to face that fear and endure that pain because he was motivated by love. He loves his family and wants to provide for them. He loves his community and wants to protect it. He loves his job and wants to do it with excellence. He loves life and wants to preserve it. That love gave him the courage to face great pain.

When I think about why God allows seasons of pain into

our lives, I think about that story. We tend to fear and worry about things the way Billy worried about the pain, but just as in his case, even though it might hurt really badly, it's usually over quickly. On top of that, Billy was given a tool he could use for the rest of his life as a result of enduring that pain. When you and I endure seasons of pain, God always uses them to develop our faith and perseverance and to give us tools that we couldn't have earned any other way.

God is not some sadistic little kid torturing insects for fun; he's the embodiment of love, and he loves you more than you can imagine. If you're in a season of difficulty, don't let fear get the best of you. Turn instead to the love of your heavenly Father and find comfort there. Even in those moments of pain, he will carry you through it and bring good from it somehow. Love has the power to overcome your fears by giving you the courage to face them with faith.

HOW LOVE CAN CHASE AWAY OUR FEARS

Whether or not you'll ever have to face a Taser, we all have areas of fear in our lives. When God created us, I think he knew how much we'd struggle with fear and how big a threat to our lives fear could become. That's why he told us over and over in the Bible, "Don't be afraid."

He didn't just tell us not to be afraid; he went a step further and told us why we didn't have to be afraid. He promised to always be with us. What a promise!

That confidence of knowing we're not alone is enough to keep our fear at bay. When my kids tell me they're scared because they think there's a monster under their beds or hiding in their closets, I tell them not to be afraid, but then I also tell them the reason why: "Your dad is right here. I love you, and I'm not going to let anything happen to you. I will beat up any monster or boogie man who tries to get into this house. I promise."

My kids look at me with some skepticism, because I'm not all that big and I'm sure the imaginary monsters are much bigger and stronger than I am. But my love, presence, and reassurance seem to eventually displace their fears. Love has the power to do that. It doesn't matter that I don't have the strength of a superhero; all that matters is that I have a super-sized amount of love for them and they know it.

LOVE CREATES COURAGE

One of the most courageous people in the Bible is a woman named Esther. There's an entire book of the Bible named for her as a tribute to her love and faith in the face of life-threatening circumstances. Her courage defined the fate of a nation.

Esther lived in a time when her nation of Israel had been exiled to Persia under the rule of a king named Xerxes. Esther's beauty caught the king's eye, and after a nationwide beauty contest resembling a twisted version of "The Bachelor," King Xerxes chose Esther to be his queen.

In the palace Esther was insulated from most of the struggles of her countrymen, until her cousin Mordecai informed her that a genocide was being planned against their people and that he believed God had put her in a position of influence with the king for this time and purpose.

Esther was forced to make a very difficult choice. Although she was the queen, the laws of the land meant she could be executed for entering the king's presence without being invited. Time was short, and she couldn't wait for him to call for her. Still, her decision to approach the king's throne could have meant instant death. (King Xerxes could have benefited from some intensive marriage counseling.)

Esther wasn't only willing to sacrifice her life; she was willing to sacrifice her lifestyle. Selfishness could have seduced her into ignoring the cries of her people as she enjoyed the comforts and opulence of palace life. Instead, she refused to remain passive in this fight. Her love for her people proved to be greater than her love for her comfort and even her love for her own life. Her heart was so full of love there was no room left for fear.

Esther called her people to a time of fasting as they united together in prayer leading up to her self-invited meeting with the king. When the period of praying and fasting ended, Esther summoned her courage and boldly entered the king's chamber. I'm sure she held her breath as she waited for the king's response.

Fortunately, the king was pleased to see her. Through a series of meetings, Esther was eventually able to leverage her influence and persuade the king to stop the travesty about to take place. She saved her people. Her courage changed history, and it was all made possible because of love.

APPLYING THE THIRD LAW OF LOVE

You've probably never had to risk your life the way Esther did, but everyone has had to overcome fears. I don't know what fears in your life have gripped you, but I know that love has the power to loosen that grip. As you look for practical ways to apply this Law of Love to your life and relationships, here are a few ways to get started. Begin applying these principles in your life, and you'll see love's influence grow stronger and fear's influence get weaker every day.

1. Be transparent.

Once I could be honest about my fear of mice, my transparency and vulnerability helped me grow closer to Ashley, and it also helped me lose some of that fear. Most fears are more serious and complex than a distaste for rodents, but this same principle applies. Be honest and transparent about your fears, and invite your loved ones to be transparent with you as well. Those conversations will create greater intimacy and weaker fears.

> I DON'T KNOW WHAT FEARS IN YOUR LIFE HAVE GRIPPED YOU, BUT I KNOW THAT LOVE HAS THE POWER TO LOOSEN THAT GRIP.

2. Trust your faith more than your feelings.

I've heard it said that FEAR is False Evidence Appearing Real. The point is that fear can cause illusions and delusions that aren't rooted in reality. We must make a conscious decision to trust the promises of God instead of the feelings brought on by our fickle minds. God's promises hold true, and he promises that he loves us and will never leave us. That alone is enough to send our fears running, because God is bigger than your biggest fear.

3. Face your fears head-on.

In the movie *Batman Begins*, we learn that Bruce Wayne was afraid of bats, and it wasn't until he was able to face that fear that he was able to become a superhero. The storyline might be a bit far-fetched, but the truth behind that principle is real. When we face our fears, we show them who's boss, and we discover a powerful inner strength.

FINAL THOUGHT

Imagine what you could accomplish if there wasn't even a hint of fear holding you back. Picture your relationships without any anxiety or worry holding you back. Envision your life with a heart full of love and courage. How does that vision look different than your life looks right now? That fearless vision is possible if you choose to live a life led by love. Commit to the path of love, and never look back to the path of fear. Great days are ahead. God promised it, so you know it's true.

DISCUSSION QUESTIONS

1. What were your biggest childhood fears?
2. What's one fear you have overcome?
3. What's one fear you're wrestling with today?
4. How has fear impacted your relationships?
5. Can you think of one example where someone's love helped you overcome a moment of fear?

CHAPTER 5

LOVE OFFERS GRACE

Make allowance for each other's faults, and forgive
anyone who offends you. Remember, the Lord forgave you,
so you must forgive others. Above all, clothe yourselves
with love, which binds us all together in perfect harmony.

—COLOSSIANS 3:13–14

One of the most popular TV movies in recent years was Lifetime's *The Client List*, which chronicled the true story of a Texas wife and mom who started making money by working as a prostitute. Her double life was finally brought to light when the brothel was raided by police and her secrets were exposed. Her husband was disgusted and shocked, and she was eventually abandoned by everyone she loved.

You might think that kind of provocative story line only happens on TV, but the Bible actually has a similar story, but with a much better ending. The Bible's version is about a man named Hosea with a wife named Gomer. Hosea loved his wife unconditionally, and that was put to the test when she abandoned her husband and family to return to her old life of prostitution.

By the time Hosea found out, they'd had several children, and he wasn't sure if any of them were his. To make matters even worse, her crimes had landed her in prison, and based on the laws of the day, her next step was to be sold into slavery to repay her debts. Hosea had every earthly right to write her off and leave her to the fate she had created for herself, but God had a different plan. God wanted to use this whole situation to show the amazing grace and unimaginable love he has for us even in those moments when we are completely unworthy.

God moved Hosea's heart toward forgiveness and compassion. Hosea went to that slave auction and took most of his life's savings to purchase back his wife. Based on the culture's legal system, she now would have had no rights at all. He would have had all the power in the relationship, and he could have used it to punish her for the rest of her life. Knowing this, she bowed her head to him and called him "Master."

What happened next is one of the most beautiful displays of grace ever recorded. In essence, he looked at her and said, "Never call me your master. I am your husband."

He gave up his rights to punish, control, or humiliate her; and instead, he welcomed her home as his wife. This simple but powerful act of forgiveness shows us a beautiful picture of the unmerited grace and love God offers to us all.

IF WE DESERVED FORGIVENESS, IT WOULDN'T BE CALLED GRACE. IF WE COULD EARN IT, IT WOULDN'T BE REAL LOVE.

I'm not sure how trust has been broken in your relationships, and I'm definitely not advocating that you give your loved ones a free pass to break your heart, because a healthy relationship must be built on trust, accountability, and mutual respect. My hope is simply that this story will open your mind and your heart a little wider to let more love and grace flow into your life.

If we deserved forgiveness, it wouldn't be called grace. If we could earn it, it wouldn't be real love.

THE PERFECT EXAMPLE OF LOVE AND GRACE

Jesus was the perfect embodiment of both love and truth. He never told a lie, but at the same time he was never cruel or judgmental with the truth. Every word he spoke was wrapped in love, so even when the truth hurt, he never broke anyone's trust.

Jesus not only modeled how to speak the truth in love, but he also showed us how to offer grace when trust is broken.

When Jesus was sentenced to death, his followers dispersed in fear of meeting the same fate. Peter, however, decided to follow Jesus on an undercover mission to see what became of his master. But when he was recognized by several people, he passionately denied ever knowing Jesus. In Jesus' moment of vulnerability, Peter betrayed him.

Crushed by his actions, Peter went away that night and wept bitter tears. He was ashamed of himself, and he was convinced that Jesus was probably ashamed of him too. Jesus died on a cross the next day, and Peter was convinced that the story was over and he'd have to live with his shame for the rest of his life.

But love always makes a way for healing.

Jesus conquered death, and after his resurrection he appeared to Peter. Against the tranquil backdrop of the sunrise, Jesus casually cooked breakfast on the shore while Peter, who was out on the water fishing, literally jumped out of the boat to get to his Savior.

When Peter got to the shore, Jesus asked him the same question three times: "Peter, do you love me?"

Each time, Peter answered, "Yes, Lord. You know that I love you."

Each time, Jesus replied, "Then feed my sheep."

Peter started to get offended by the third time of being asked the same question, but what he didn't see in the moment was that Jesus was showing him love has the power to cover over our sins. Peter denied Jesus three times, and now, Jesus was extending the grace to allow Peter to affirm his love three times.

Jesus didn't just pat him on the back and commend him for giving the right answer. He called Peter to a life of love and leadership in the church. Peter, an uneducated fisherman who had denied his Savior three times, was being commissioned to become a great leader in a movement that would change the world for eternity. The unmerited grace Peter received from Jesus propelled him into a life of extraordinary influence and, ultimately, courageous martyrdom for the cause of Christ.

WE CAN'T RECEIVE GOD'S GRACE WITHOUT BEING WILLING TO EXTEND GRACE TO OTHERS.

Jesus loved Peter enough to give him the opportunity to be forgiven and rebuild trust. That opportunity for grace wasn't an exclusive offer for Peter; it's an opportunity God freely extends to all of us who have broken trust (which is everybody). It's also a command. We can't receive God's grace without being willing to extend grace to others.

GRUDGES ARE LIKE MOSQUITOS

In the South the summers are hot and the mosquitoes aggressive. Our Georgia mosquitoes seem to love me a lot more than they love my sweet wife. Ashley hardly ever gets bitten, but every time I walk outside, I get swarmed. I spend most of my summers indoors scratching my mosquito bites.

I'm not sure how mosquitoes communicate with each other, but I'm convinced that they have their own language and have all told one another about me. I can picture them buzzing around the old watering hole and saying, "Hey, have you tasted the guy who lives in that house? He's delicious! Let's meet at his place for Happy Hour. He's got the best blood in the neighborhood!"

I'm not sure why I'm so delicious, but I wish I weren't. Being so popular with the mosquitoes is no fun, so I've had to invest in a high-powered DEET mosquito repellent, which was specially formulated by the US military to help keep pesky bugs off of servicemen and women serving in locations around the world where bugs are rampant. The DEET seems to work well, and even though I smell like a chemical factory after putting it on, the mosquitoes leave me alone.

I share this mosquito story because our lack of forgiveness, like mosquitoes, can cause a lot of frustration in our lives, but there's a repellent to stop them. Our old grudges can swarm around in our brains and cause perpetual distraction and discomfort, which rob us of joy in our relationships. The repellent for grudges can't be sprayed on like DEET; it must be applied through a life of love. Simply put, love has the power to repel our hard-hearted, stubborn refusal to forgive.

FORGIVENESS VERSUS TRUST

Some people get stuck in a cycle of grudges and mistrust because they wrongly assume that forgiveness and trust are the same thing.

It's vital that we understand their distinctions. Forgiveness can't be earned; it can only be given freely. That's why it's called grace. Trust, however, can't be given freely; it can only be earned.

When someone breaks your trust, you should give your forgiveness instantly, but give your trust slowly as it is earned through consistency of actions by whoever broke your trust. During this period of rebuilding, fight the urge to punish or retaliate. Those actions won't do anything to promote healing, and healing always needs to be our ultimate objective. Love, after all, is a healing force.

> YOU DON'T HAVE TO TRUST SOMEONE IN ORDER TO FORGIVE, BUT YOU DO HAVE TO FORGIVE SOMEONE IN ORDER TO MAKE TRUST POSSIBLE AGAIN.

You don't have to trust someone in order to forgive, but you do have to forgive someone in order to make trust possible again.

REBUILDING TRUST

One of the most common questions I hear is the question of how to rebuild trust once it has been broken. This is a very tough issue, but it's vital to understand if we're going to have healthy relationships. Trust is the foundation of love, and once the foundation has been cracked, it must be repaired or the relationship will crumble.

When you've broken trust, you must be willing to take immediate action to rebuild it. When someone has broken your trust, you must be willing to provide that person the opportunity to rebuild. Giving someone the chance to reestablish trust is one of the most loving acts you can do for someone.

My two older boys have both broken their arms before, but please don't call Child Protective Services on me! I had nothing to do with either accident. One of the arm breaks actually happened while I was preaching a sermon at our church and my four-year-old son dove off a rocking chair in the toddler room. My boys are all stuntmen-in-training.

In both incidents, when we put a cast on and repeated the doctor's orders to stop roughhousing for a while, the boys acted like I was inflicting a cruel punishment on them. I tried to explain that the casts and the precautions weren't there for punishment but rather to promote healing.

At first, the boys couldn't seem to see past their discomfort. They couldn't see the bigger picture. They didn't understand how these uncomfortable limitations were actually for their benefit.

The cast limited their mobility, but it also protected the mending bone. The rules to temporarily give up certain freedoms and restrict certain motions were also in place to prevent any further damage to the break, so the arm could become stronger than it ever was before. But if the boys refused to follow the prescribed path to healing, their arms might never heal properly.

In a similar way, when trust has been broken in a relationship, the person who broke the trust must be willing to temporarily give up certain freedoms over a period of time to promote healing. For instance, if a husband lies to his wife about their financial situation and how he's spending money, then rebuilding trust will probably require him to willingly give up certain freedoms with spending. He may need to keep every receipt for a while and check in with his wife before making any purchase. This may seem drastic or it might feel like a punishment or a blow to his pride, but these self-imposed restraints can be a vital aspect of the healing process.

Another example might involve a teenage daughter who stays out an hour past curfew without checking in. The parents may choose to impose certain restraints, including a period of being grounded followed by a period of having an earlier curfew with frequent check-in phone calls. In this situation, the parent-enforced sanctions are technically punishments, but their ultimate purpose is to create an opportunity for trust to be rebuilt and healthy habits to be reestablished.

> THE PROCESS OF REBUILDING TRUST MIGHT BE SLOW AND IT MIGHT BE PAINFUL, BUT IT'S WORTH IT.

The process of rebuilding trust might be slow and it might be painful, but it's worth it. Once you've worked through your issues and established trust, your relationship can become stronger and more vibrant than it ever was before.

BEYOND FORGIVENESS

Have you ever experienced a betrayal in your own life or witnessed a travesty in the life of someone else and thought to yourself, *That's simply beyond forgiveness. I can forgive up to a certain point, but I could never forgive something like that.*

There's a sense of justice within us that can be offended by grace. After all, when someone wrongs us, that person should be punished, right?

These are important questions, and they're far too important to answer with mere opinion. We need to look straight to God's Word, because he is not only the creator of love, he's also the creator of grace.

One of the longest narratives recorded in the Bible is found in the book of Genesis. There we're introduced to a character named Jacob, who had twelve sons. Jacob's name was eventually changed to Israel, and his sons became the patriarchs of the twelve tribes of Israel.

Jacob was a hero of the faith, but he was far from perfect. His polygamist lifestyle and his dysfunctional approach to parenting created insecurity and unhealthy competition among his sons. Eventually, Joseph emerged as a favorite of his father. Jacob would give special gifts and recognitions to Joseph, and the brothers hated Joseph for it.

One day, Joseph was telling his brothers about a dream he'd had where they were all bowing down to him. It proved to be the breaking point for the jealous siblings. They threw Joseph into an abandoned well and started plotting the best way to make him disappear permanently.

Several of the brothers wanted to kill him, but then they decided they might as well profit from him instead. A band of foreigners was traveling past on their way to Egypt, so the brothers hoisted Joseph out of the well and sold him to the foreigners. They covered up their crime by putting animal blood all over Joseph's coat and bringing it home to their father.

Sold into slavery by his brothers. I don't know what kind of heartbreak you've experienced in your life, but I doubt many of us have experienced that level of betrayal.

The heartbreaking grief nearly killed Jacob. He pledged to mourn the loss of his son for the rest of his life.

Joseph was seventeen years old when he was placed on an auction block and sold to an Egyptian official named Potiphar. The young slave was taken to his new home in shackles. His dreams were shattered. His life would never be the same.

Joseph could have allowed bitterness and resentment to take

root in his heart. He could have replayed his brothers' crime over and over in his mind. He could have given up and ended his own life. He didn't do any of those things. Instead, he chose to trust God and make the most of his situation.

Joseph started working hard and earning his master's trust. It wasn't long before Joseph was placed in charge of the entire estate. His work ethic had earned the respect of everyone in the house. Life was going as well as it could go for a young man with no freedom.

But Joseph's story was about to take a dramatic twist. Potiphar's wife took notice of the handsome young slave, and she began trying to seduce him. Joseph could have justified giving in to her advances and satisfying his own natural drives, but he refused to dishonor his God or his earthly master in such a way. He repeatedly refused to give in to the temptation.

She gradually grew furious at his repeated rejections and decided to punish him for it. She told her husband that Joseph had tried to rape her, and Joseph was thrown into a dungeon as a result.

At this point, I think most of us would have completely given up hope. We may have lost all faith in God's goodness. Joseph could have said, "God, if you're out there, you obviously don't care about me. I've done everything I can do to live my life with honor and faith, and I've been betrayed over and over. I've gone from being a free man to a slave and now a prisoner. It's all my brothers's fault. I'll never forgive them for ruining my life!"

Joseph didn't take that approach. Instead, he decided to trust God as best he could from within the prison walls. He assumed that if God was allowing him to be in this prison, it must be for a good reason as part of a bigger plan. Joseph kept his faith. He refused to allow bitterness to take root in his heart. He refused to hate his brothers or his accusers or anyone else.

It wasn't long before Joseph had won the warden's respect and was given freedom to run the entire prison under the warden's supervision. Joseph made the most of a bad situation. He also used his unique, God-given ability to interpret dreams. He deciphered the hidden messages God communicated to the other inmates while they slept. Joseph's unshakable faith in God changed the culture of the prison and encouraged men who had lost all hope.

After seven years as a slave and seven more years as a prisoner, Joseph received a life-changing opportunity. The pharaoh, the sovereign leader of Egypt, was being tormented by dreams no one could interpret. Joseph's reputation had grown beyond the prison walls, and Pharaoh called on the prisoner to make sense of his dreams.

Joseph told Pharaoh that God was telling him what was about to happen in Egypt. A period of great abundance would soon come to Egypt followed by a period of severe famine. If preparations weren't made and food systematically stored during the good years, Egypt would starve during the famine.

Pharaoh saw the wisdom and confidence in the young prisoner before him and appointed him governor over all of Egypt. Joseph would be in charge of the empire, and he would be second-in-command to Pharaoh.

That's quite a turn of events! Joseph was promoted from the bottom rung on the social ladder to the very top within a matter of minutes—a God-given opportunity made possible because of Joseph's faithfulness during the difficult years. Our responses to present difficulties will often determine our level of future opportunities.

Fast-forward to the famine. Joseph was ruling well and had earned the respect of a grateful nation. Not only did Egypt have enough stored food for the Egyptians, but foreigners were traveling from different lands to purchase food. In a moment of poetic justice, Joseph's brothers ended up standing before him to buy food and bowing at his feet. It was the image he had dreamed would happen decades earlier.

His brothers didn't recognize him. They were convinced he was dead, and they had lived with unspeakable guilt all these years. Joseph put his brothers through a series of tests to measure their current level of integrity, and when he could stand it no longer, he revealed himself.

Joseph was overcome with emotion, and his brothers were overcome with terror. They believed they were about to face divine retribution and execution for their terrible crime. What they experienced instead was unmerited, radical grace. At the end of this ordeal, Joseph spoke some of the most profound and grace-filled words recorded in the Bible:

> "You intended to harm me, but God intended it all for good. He brought me to this position so I could save the lives of many people. No, don't be afraid. I will continue to take care of you and your children." So he reassured them by speaking kindly to them (Gen. 50: 20–21).

Joseph forgave his brothers. Not only did he forgive them, but he encouraged them so that they would not continue to punish themselves for what they had done to him so many years ago. They had meant it all for evil, but God had been working in this plan all along and meant it all for good. He used the ordeal to teach them all lessons of grace and the faithfulness of God.

Had Joseph executed his brothers, the nation of Israel would have died before it even began. Instead, a family was reborn and a nation was established all because of grace. Love won.

YOUR STORY OF GRACE

I don't know what you've been through. I don't know how you've been hurt or how you've been betrayed, and I don't know what you've done to hurt and betray others. What I do know is that God loves you. God offers his grace to you, and he wants you to embrace his grace and then freely share it with others.

Imagine what your relationships could look like if all the drama, bitterness, and regret were replaced with grace. It's possible! It can begin with you. Have the courage to forgive yourself, and have the grace to forgive others. Once grace flows into broken hearts, love will always bring healing.

> GOD OFFERS HIS GRACE TO YOU, AND HE WANTS YOU TO EMBRACE HIS GRACE AND THEN FREELY SHARE IT WITH OTHERS.

DISCUSSION QUESTIONS

1. When was the first time you remember asking someone for forgiveness? What happened as a result?
2. When was the last time someone asked for your forgiveness? How did you respond?
3. What's the most radical example of grace you've seen?

4. Why do you think our instinct to punish can sometimes feel stronger than our instinct to forgive?
5. How would your relationships look different if everyone involved freely forgave one another?

CHAPTER 6

LOVE BRINGS HEALING

*Most important of all, continue to show deep love for
each other, for love covers a multitude of sins.*

—1 PETER 4:8

When I was in the eighth grade, I had a crush on a girl in my class named Angie. I was a pretty dorky kid in middle school, but despite my adolescent awkwardness, I managed to summon the courage to start conversations with her whenever I could. My so-called courage was actually just a combination of raging hormones and unrealistic optimism, but it felt like courage in my eighth-grade brain, and that was good enough for me.

My voice would crack and my palms would get sweaty, but with each conversation she would politely smile while she dodged the tiny spit particles flying off my braces as I spoke. I interpreted her smile to mean that she wanted to spend the rest of her life with me. We had never actually had a conversation that lasted more than thirty seconds, but I was pretty sure she was my soul mate. I was convinced that when she looked at me, she didn't see my braces and acne; she saw Prince Charming.

Our love story was off to a stellar start until the fateful day when everything would unravel in one of the most terrifying moments of my life. We were standing in science class, where I had cornered her for a chat, when I suddenly felt a draft of air on my legs. I heard laughter behind me, and Angie's face turned a bright shade of red. She covered her face and giggled and quickly ran off, leaving me standing there trying to figure out what had just happened. I looked down slowly, and to my horror, my sweatpants were down at my ankles.

Yes, I wore sweatpants to school, but don't judge me! They were comfortable, and in the early nineties in central Kentucky, they were still a socially acceptable wardrobe option for middle school. That was, however, the last day I ever wore sweatpants anywhere. You just can't trust the drawstring on those things.

This particular wardrobe malfunction, though, was not the result of a faulty drawstring; this was an act of sabotage. My "friend" Nick had grabbed my pants from behind and yanked them to the floor. God had mercy on me that day and some- how kept my Fruit of the Loom underwear from making the trip along with my pants. Had my tighty whiteys gone to the floor, too, I'd probably still be in counseling over the whole ordeal.

I pulled my pants back up to my waist with ninja-like reflexes, but the damage had been done. Humiliation had been inflicted. I had been in the most vulnerable and exposed position possible, and instead of receiving compassion and encourage- ment from this girl I really liked, I felt the sting of rejection. We never really talked after that, but it was probably more because of my own embarrassment than anything else.

MOVING FORWARD FROM PAST PAIN

I share this funny story not because it's an example of true rejection, but because it paints the picture of vulnerability in relationships and how our view of love can be shaped by our past experiences. Love requires vulnerability, and when we feel like we've been in an exposed position and then experienced rejection, our defense mechanisms can actually work against us and sabotage our current relationships.

We tend to militantly safeguard certain parts of ourselves in order to prevent the same kind of humiliation or rejection we have felt in the past. I know I wore a belt very tightly for years after that sweatpants incident.

We've all faced many relational challenges far more significant than an embarrassing middle-school prank. When we've been rejected, abandoned, or abused by the very people who should have been protecting us, the ramifications can be deep and long lasting. If you've experienced the sting of betrayal by a close friend, a parent, a sibling, or even a spouse, you know exactly the kind of pain I'm talking about.

The more you love someone, the more ability that person will have to hurt you; but until you give a person the ability to hurt you (vulnerability), you'll never be able to truly experience love. This reality keeps some people from wholeheartedly committing to a relationship, because they're trying to protect their hearts from being wounded again. But if we're not careful, our wounds from the past can create new wounds in the present. It is a catch-22 that can keep us in perpetual dysfunction in our relationships until

> IF WE'RE NOT CAREFUL, OUR WOUNDS FROM THE PAST CAN CREATE NEW WOUNDS IN THE PRESENT.

we become intentional about healing from the past and moving forward in a healthy way.

IDENTIFYING YOUR OWN
BURNS FROM THE PAST

As I interact with people who have experienced childhood abuse, marital infidelity, or any form of pain from the past, I've noticed many develop a defense mechanism I call "emotional sunburn."

Have you ever gone to the beach and forgotten to apply sunscreen? I used to live in Florida, and this would happen to me all the time. I'd think it wasn't a big deal because I'd only be exposed to the sun for a short time, but hours later, my unprotected torso would be lobster red. I'd quickly put on a T-shirt to cover my sensitive skin, but without fail, someone in my family would come give me a slap on the back or a hug that was a little too rough and I would scream in pain.

Sometimes I'd turn ugly, but we can all get ugly when we're hurting. The person touching my back wasn't trying to hurt me; the pain was from a situation he or she did nothing to cause. It was a result of my own injury and subsequent hypersensitivity. Still, that person's touch had inflicted pain because it exposed a wound that needed healing. Instead of allowing that person to rub aloe on me to promote healing, I usually retreated into solitude where I could be grumpy and alone and nobody could hurt me anymore.

In a similar way, I believe many of us have sunburn all over our hearts from being burned in our pasts. These past wounds, if left untreated, can cause us to overreact in unhealthy ways to our loved ones, pushing others away in an attempt to protect ourselves. Sometimes we even fall into a cycle of inflicting wounds on ourselves to push others away or to feel a sense of control when our lives or relationships feel out of control.

Working with youth, I've seen the tragic cycle of self-inflicted pain in the form of eating disorders or cutting, where young people (usually adolescent girls) will literally cut themselves with a blade. Many psychologists believe these actions are an attempt to regain control when their relationships at home or at school have become dysfunctional and out of control. It's a harmful cycle that creates more pain instead of healing.

These kinds of behaviors aren't a new phenomenon. In fact, the expression "cutting off your nose to spite your face" originates from a historical account of a medieval nun who famously encouraged self-mutilation as a means of self-preservation. Ebba the Younger was a ninth-century nun at a convent in Europe during a time when Vikings from the north were pillaging the land. A group of these Vikings were attempting to break into Ebba's convent one night, so she decided to take drastic action to protect her chastity from what she believed was an imminent sexual assault.

She went to the kitchen and found a knife and went to work sawing off her nose and her upper lip, leaving a bloody, grotesque sight. She encouraged all the other women to follow her example, and each nun took a knife and performed this painful act of self-mutilation. When the Vikings finally broke through the outer doors and found the nuns, the men were so horrified by the sight that they burned down the convent, killing all the women inside.

I recognize that this story is probably more of an interesting anecdote from history than a practical lesson in modern relationships. I doubt you've ever been so brokenhearted or afraid that sawing off your nose and upper lip seemed like the best possible course of action. Still, I believe this paints a vivid picture of the drastic measures people are capable of taking to protect themselves from potential pain or heartbreak even when they harm themselves in the process.

Sometimes we can subconsciously do things to make ourselves seem ugly or intimidating to drive people away, because we're afraid if we let others close to us, we'll only be hurt again. This kind of behavior might give us the illusion of power and safety that comes from isolation, but it will also hold us captive in a prison of solitude where we never experience true love.

> WHATEVER YOU MAY HAVE DONE OR WHATEVER MAY HAVE BEEN DONE TO WOUND YOU IN THE PAST, HEALING IS POSSIBLE.

Whatever you may have done or whatever may have been done to wound you in the past, healing is possible. God wants you to live a life of love. He wants you to experience rich, meaningful relationships. He wants to bring you to a place of healing so you can experience life and love in all of its fullness.

MAKING ROOM FOR HEALING

There's a show on TV called *Hoarders*. It's about people who accumulate junk and never get rid of it. Their homes are filled with piles of trash so high that the only creatures who can navigate around are roaches and rats. My dorm rooms used to look kind of like that. The show is both sad and disgusting. On a spiritual level, I think a lot of us live our lives as hoarders.

We don't mean to become hoarders; it just naturally happens over time until one day, we're buried under a pile of junk. We've got to be willing to clear away negative things that are taking up space to make room for new things that will bring peace back into our lives. Once we make these choices, we'll be in a position to help others find healing as well.

In Colossians 3, the Bible paints a picture of some of the junk that's taking up too much space in our minds, hearts, and lives: "But now is the time to get rid of anger, rage, malicious behavior, slander, and dirty language" (v. 8).

We can't get rid of this kind of junk by throwing it in a garbage bag. We need to pray for God to remove it and be willing to drastically change our attitudes, behaviors, and decisions to push the remnants of these negative things out of our lives. Once they start to clear away, it's time to bring in new things to replace them, and just a few verses later the Bible tells us what those new things should be: "Since God chose you to be the holy people he loves, you must clothe yourselves with tenderhearted mercy, kindness, humility, gentleness, and patience" (Col. 3:12).

These aren't things we can pick up at the mall. Again, we need to ask God to fill our lives with these attributes and be diligent in our efforts to hold onto them. We must allow God's Word to renew our minds and give us a new way of thinking that leads to a new way of living.

He wants to bring you healing. Trust him enough to let go of those things that are holding you back. Those are toxic forces sabotaging your relationships. Once you have the faith to let go of the junk, your hands and your heart will be open to receive healing.

Keep in mind that this isn't a one-time process. The negative clutter has a tendency to keep working its way into our lives, so this should become a lifestyle pattern of clearing out the old (negative stuff) and making room for the new (positive stuff). Don't let yourself get buried by negativity. Let love sweep through your life, and replace that junk with joy.

HOW TO HEAL

We've all had pain. Perhaps you have lived in perpetual pain inflicted over a lifetime of abuse and betrayal by those you loved most, or perhaps you've been fortunate to have relatively few moments of heartbreak. Either way, none of us is immune to pain from the past, and all of us can benefit from healing. The health of your present and future relationships may hinge on how you choose to address the issue of healing in your past.

Healing looks different at different stages in the process, but I want to start by addressing those who are in a current crisis and need some critical care. When we're hurt, isolated, or angry, we tend to make our worst decisions; so in the midst of the storm you're in right now, please let me give you some perspective. The decisions you'll make in the days to come might set the trajectory for the next chapter of your life.

> THE DECISIONS YOU'LL MAKE IN THE DAYS TO COME MIGHT SET THE TRAJECTORY FOR THE NEXT CHAPTER OF YOUR LIFE.

There are so many examples I could share of people who have endured unimaginable heartbreak, but one compelling story that jumps to mind is the journey of my dear friends Jay and Mandra. They are a remarkable example of faith and perseverance in the midst of unimaginable tragedy. Their lives were changed forever in a single moment. I shared part of their story in my previous book *iVow: Secrets to a Stronger Marriage* as an extraordinary example of how a couple can remain committed "for better or for worse."

I remember getting the phone call that night. I was at a flag football practice for my son Cooper. The voice on the line was a deputy sheriff telling me that I needed to get to the hospital right away because there had been an accident. Trying to control his own emotions, the deputy told me the details, and with a sick feeling in my stomach, I started praying some desperate prayers as I drove Cooper home and rushed to the emergency room.

I broke multiple traffic laws getting to the hospital. When I arrived, I sprinted from the parking lot into the waiting room and tried to regain my composure and control my heart rate before anyone saw me. I caught my breath and told the receptionist that I was a pastor and friend of the Kerns family, and with a sad and solemn tone in her voice, she pointed me to a private waiting room where Jay and Mandra were waiting.

Jay is one of the biggest and strongest people I know. He had singlehandedly carried my wife's piano when we moved into our home a few months earlier, but in that moment, Jay looked powerless. His mighty shoulders were slumped in despair. Mandra sat motionless by his side with an expression of disbelief on her face. The couple looked as if they had aged a decade in the few days since I had seen them last.

I gave them both a hug, and we all sat down. With trembling voices, they began to tell me the details of what had happened that night.

Mandra had been out running errands, and Jay stayed home to watch their three young kids. Jay was playing in the backyard with his four-year-old daughter, Jayden, while also keeping an eye on their two-year-old and holding their baby boy. The baby's diaper needed changing, so Jay asked Jayden if she wanted to stay and play in the backyard while he changed the diaper. She said yes, so Jay and the younger two kids went into the house.

Jay returned to the backyard a few minutes later, but he didn't see Jayden anywhere. He called her name a few times, but there was no answer. He thought that she might have walked into the house, so he went inside calling her name, but there was no answer. He started to get a little bit concerned. He went next door where she sometimes played with a neighbor, but they hadn't seen her.

Jay paused to gather his thoughts, and in a moment of terror, he realized there was one place he hadn't thought to look. He hadn't considered it as a possibility because Jayden was always so careful to stay away from it. She knew not to go near it without an adult, but maybe something had happened and she had fallen in. In the most terrifying moment of his life, Jay ran to the backyard while pleading with God. He stopped and held his breath as he peered over the edge of their swimming pool.

He was begging God that she wouldn't be there as he looked through the autumn leaves that covered the surface of the water. Then he saw his daughter lying on the floor of the pool. He dove in and pulled her out. It was the darkest moment of his life.

The minutes that followed were a blur. There was CPR and frantic screams for help and police and ambulances. Finally, the chaos was replaced with an eerie stillness in a sterile waiting room.

We sat in that room and waited. It didn't seem real.

We prayed for the best and tried to brace ourselves for the worst. In a moment like that, many mothers would lash out in anger. Some would have expected Mandra to scream at Jay and blame him for this tragedy, but what she did instead was a picture of grace. With tears in her eyes, she summoned her strength to support her husband in his most fragile moment.

She kept rubbing his back and whispering words of love and affirmation to him. She would softly say, "I love you so much. You are such a good dad. This isn't your fault. This could have happened to anyone. God is going to carry us through this. No matter what happens, we're going to face this together. I love you so much."

They were living out their marriage vow to love "for better or for worse" in a powerful way. I knew that whatever news walked through that waiting room door, my friends would make it. Their faith in God and their commitment to each other was unshakable.

A few minutes later, a doctor walked in with a chaplain standing beside him. The doctor began a well-rehearsed speech with an inevitably tragic ending. They had done everything they could do, but Jayden was gone.

The pain was overwhelming, and yet, there was a peace in that waiting room that can't be explained apart from the presence of God himself. The Prince of Peace was holding the parents of that precious little girl. He was giving them peace in their darkest moment. He was comforting them with the hope of knowing that he would never leave their sides and their daughter was safe in the arms of her Savior.

It was a holy moment. It's a moment I would never want to relive, and yet, I'm eternally thankful that I was able to be present in it. Through our tears, I was reminded of the shortest verse in the Bible which simply says, "Jesus wept."

I find so much comfort in knowing that our God is not distant from us in our times of pain and heartbreak. He's not indifferent to our suffering. He is not emotionless. He is present with us in our pain, and his love has the power to carry us through the storm.

The days that followed Jayden's tragic passing were filled with tears but also filled with hope. Jay and Mandra cried many tears, but they also chose to thank God for the time they had been blessed with their daughter. They also thanked God that Jayden wasn't truly gone. She was with Jesus, and they celebrated the fact that in Christ no good-bye is ever final.

> HE IS PRESENT WITH US IN OUR PAIN, AND HIS LOVE HAS THE POWER TO CARRY US THROUGH THE STORM.

Jayden's life on earth was short, but her impact was huge. We hosted a funeral at our church and another celebration of her life at her preschool. At both ceremonies, two of her favorite songs were sung. One was "Over the Rainbow," and the other was a worship anthem called "Mighty to Save."

Even in death, Jayden's pure faith, joyful spirit, and unbridled love continue to touch hearts. Many people have come to faith in Christ as a direct result of Jayden's legacy. She was on earth only four years, but her impact will be felt for eternity.

THE CROSSROADS OF PAIN

I pray you never have to experience the kind of tragedy Jay and Mandra experienced, but on some level, every person will experience loss. In those moments of heartbreak, you'll find yourself standing at a critical crossroads.

One choice will lead you down a path of bitterness. You'll be tempted to push loved ones away. You might even be tempted to push God away because you blame him for the pain you are experiencing. The path of bitterness might feel liberating at first, but it will prove to be a trap in the end.

The other path is a road to healing. It's a road where you choose to trust God even when you don't understand what's happening. It's a road where you'll be willing to use your own pain as a way to help others find healing, which will ultimately help you find healing too.

This path of healing is the one Jay and Mandra chose to follow. They continue to celebrate Jayden's life and legacy, and they share their own story as a way to give strength and hope to people all over the world. I'm honored to call them my friends, and I hope that if I ever experience a similar tragedy, I will have the faith to respond the way they have responded.

HAVE FAITH IN THE HEALER

I don't believe it's possible to have peace after a loss like Jay and Mandra's without faith in God's presence and provision. Jay and Mandra wisely understand that real peace isn't the absence of tragedy but the presence of a Savior who is bigger than your tragedy. Healing from a broken heart isn't the result of mere time and effort. It comes when we put our trust in the healer of our hearts.

> REAL PEACE ISN'T THE ABSENCE OF TRAGEDY BUT THE PRESENCE OF A SAVIOR WHO IS BIGGER THAN YOUR TRAGEDY.

Jesus was the physical embodiment of love, so it makes sense that he was also the embodiment of healing. Everywhere he went, he loved people and he healed people using two primary methods: his words and his touch.

We can do the same to promote love and healing in our own relationships.

Be willing to speak a kind word to the loved one in your life who needs encouragement today. Send an encouraging text message or, better yet, pick up the phone and call. Don't let your love be an unspoken assumption. Make sure your loved ones know exactly how much you love them because your words and actions make it clear.

Jesus gave us many examples of his healing power in the Bible. One of the most famous encounters involved a woman who had been suffering from bleeding for many years. Her condition was not only painful, but culturally it also ostracized her from society. She was suffering both physically and relationally. An encounter with Jesus would change everything for her: Jesus provided the healing she needed, but he didn't just heal her body. His love healed her soul. He reaffirmed her humanity. He reminded her of her limitless worth. He addressed her as an adopted member of his own family. He healed her with a touch and also with his words: "And he said to her, 'Daughter, your faith has made you well. Go in peace. Your suffering is over'" (Mark 5:34).

Healing flows from relationships. Jesus addressed this woman as a "daughter" to remind her that God was not distant from her. She was part of God's family. Jesus cared about her physical need, but he also took time to address her relational need. He does the same for you and me.

An encounter with Jesus always has the power to bring healing. When love is present, healing is present. It won't always look miraculous, but it will always make a difference.

I believe that most of us want to experience a supernatural encounter with Jesus. We want healing (physical, financial, emotional, and spiritual) in our own lives, but we don't always know how to receive these gifts that Jesus freely offers to us. Below is a simple outline to follow. Remember, Jesus is not a genie in a bottle or a vending machine that exists to give you what you think you want. He is your loving Savior whose plans for your life are much better than your own.

The healing that love brings might not always look like you think it should, but in the scope of eternity, it will prove to be exactly what you need for your good and God's glory. When you're ready to embrace healing in your own life and also are willing to be a conduit for God's healing in others, here are a few keys to keep in mind:

Believe in God's power.

Love brings healing, but it's never through our own power. It's always a result of God's power. We're vessels of love, but the true source is God himself, and he's also the source of real and lasting healing. Putting your faith and trust in him is the first step.

> "And it is impossible to please God without faith. Anyone who wants to come to him must believe that God exists and that he rewards those who sincerely seek him" (Heb. 11:6).

Pray with faith.

Anything worth worrying about is worth praying about. When you want to experience healing in your life or the life of a loved one, ask God for it. Sometimes God uses prayer to change the situation, and sometimes he uses prayer to change our own perspective about the situation, but either way, he's always doing something positive through prayer.

"Don't worry about anything; instead, pray about everything. Tell God what you need, and thank him for all he has done. Then you will experience God's peace, which exceeds anything we can understand. His peace will guard your hearts and minds as you live in Christ Jesus" (Phil. 4:6–7).

Trust God no matter what.

God has a purpose for your pain, a reason for your struggles, and a reward for your faithfulness. Trust him, and don't give up! Don't base your faith merely on the outcome of your prayers. Base your faith on what God has already done to love you and save you. We usually won't see how the plans all fit together on this side of eternity, but he's promised us a home in heaven where his love and healing will be perfectly experienced forever.

"Trust in the LORD with all your heart; do not depend on your own understanding. Seek his will in all you do, and he will show you which path to take" (Prov. 3:5–6).

DISCUSSION QUESTIONS

1. If you could bring healing to one part of your health or your life, which part would you choose?
2. Have you ever experienced an emotional, spiritual, or physical healing as a result of love?
3. Do you believe God still performs miracles? Why or why not?
4. What's one relationship in your life where you have the power to help promote healing through your love and encouragement?

CHAPTER 7

LOVE LIVES FOREVER

Three things will last forever—faith, hope, and love—and the greatest of these is love.

—1 CORINTHIANS 13:13

I've always been a bit of a prankster. Perhaps it's because my sense of humor never matured much beyond adolescence, but whatever the reason, I can rarely resist the opportunity to pull a prank on a friend or relative.

One of the most epic pranks I ever pulled off took a team of people working behind the scenes to make it happen. Two of our pastors, Marty and Todd, were having major milestone birthdays in the same week. Marty was turning fifty years old, and Todd was turning forty.

A small team of fellow pranksters and I started working together to hatch a plan to surprise them both. Marty and Todd were most likely expecting a surprise party, so we knew that if we were actually going to surprise them, then this party had to be something completely unexpected. We threw out all kinds of ideas until the granddaddy of all pranks was finally birthed.

It was unprecedented. It was epic. It was ridiculous. It was dangerous. It was everything we loved in a potential prank. We were going to stage a fake funeral.

I know how tacky it sounds, and you're right. It *was* tacky. But it was also fun! We were determined to put the "fun" back in "funeral."

The stakes were high, because not only were we going to great lengths to fabricate a fake death, but we were also pranking two pastors who were the bosses of almost everyone directly involved. I'm pretty sure all of us updated our résumés the week before the party, just in case things went sour. We decided that the potential job loss was worth the risk.

A woman in our church named Pat agreed to be the grieving relative of her young cousin who had tragically and unexpectedly died. Her young cousin, by the way, was in on the prank and actually agreed to fake his death on social media. Don't worry, he told all his relatives and friends the truth ahead of time. Still, this was an incredibly elaborate con.

The day of the funeral came around. I was officiating the ceremony, and I was so nervous I was feeling nauseous all morning. The hearse was parked outside, the auditorium was set up with pictures, and the grieving churchgoers started streaming into the auditorium. Some of those folks could have won Academy Awards for how much they were playing it up.

The ceremony started, and Pat asked Marty if he would join her onstage as she said a few words about her dead cousin. This seemed like an odd request, but it's hard to say no to a grieving relative at a funeral, so Marty politely obliged and joined her onstage. You could have cut the awkward tension with a knife.

Finally, everyone was in place. Todd was already onstage strumming a guitar lightly to set a somber, respectful tone as a prelude to the ceremony. He had no idea that he was playing at his own funeral.

I looked around, and realizing the gravity and the absurdity of the situation, I was frozen. I couldn't think of what to say or do next. My life flashed before my eyes, and I wondered if this would be the prank that caused a real funeral for me.

I awkwardly welcomed the assembly of fake mourners and then stumbled through an introduction. Finally, I got to the moment of truth. I said, "We've all come here today for a celebration, and the real reason we're here isn't because of a death. It's because of you two guys! Happy birthday, Marty and Todd!"

The crowd erupted with applause and laughter. Pat reached into the urn supposedly holding the ashes of her dead cousin and pulled out confetti, which she threw on the birthday boys. Even I was surprised by that colorful detail.

The birthday boys stood there with stunned shock and sheepish smiles on their faces. When we all finally regained our composure, we put Marty and Todd's pictures on the side screens with their years of birth and a hyphen. It was the kind of picture you'd use in an actual funeral.

With their pictures on the big screens, we brought out friends and relatives who took turns talking about Marty and Todd. We shared funny stories, but we also shared touching tributes to these great men, wonderful pastors, and extraordinary friends.

It's sad, but oftentimes, we wait until someone has died before we share all the things we love about the person. These guys got the rare gift of being able to sit in the front row at their own funerals, and they were able to hear the words of adoration first-hand. It was a very memorable day. The birthday boys even got to ride in the hearse on the way to lunch afterward.

I don't think Marty and Todd enjoyed the fake funeral nearly as much as the rest of us, but none of us lost our jobs that day so I still count it as a big win.

FUN AT A FUNERAL

As a Christian, I believe you should be able to have fun at a funeral. Even real ones. We can celebrate because we know that death isn't the end of the story.

One of my favorite stories in the Bible took place at a funeral. The story started with tears, but it ended with laughter. The scene was a funeral processional.

They didn't travel by hearse back then. The crowd of mourners walked through the street holding a bier with the body of a young man who had died too soon. His grieving mother was right next to her son's corpse. I'm sure she felt as if her life were over too.

Not only was this woman experiencing the unimaginable heartbreak of burying a child, but she was also facing the reality of having no one left. The culture at this time was inhospitable to women and to widows specifically. There were few legitimate options for a woman seeking employment, and there was no government assistance. Family was expected to provide all the care, and if a husband wasn't around, then the responsibility fell to her sons.

This grieving mother wasn't just burying her child; in many ways she was burying her future.

Jesus and his followers were coming down the same road, and when the two crowds met, it was a recipe for a miracle. Jesus brought the boy back to life and gave him back to his mother. Tears instantly turned to joy. A funeral became a party.

A lot of people's lives mirror that same story line. They might start out with tears and difficulties, but they can still end with joy and laughter. Whenever God is the one writing the story, you can be sure there'll be a happy ending.

This doesn't mean there's never a time to grieve. God gave tears as a healthy emotional response to pain and loss. Jesus cried when his friend Lazarus died. He cried even while knowing he was about to bring Lazarus back from the dead. When you've experienced loss or tragedy, don't be afraid to grieve, but don't stay in your grief too long.

> WHENEVER GOD IS THE ONE WRITING THE STORY, YOU CAN BE SURE THERE'LL BE A HAPPY ENDING.

Grief is kind of like a sauna. It can be healthy and beneficial if we stay there for short periods of time, but it can be dangerous or even deadly if we stay there too long. We don't grieve as those who have no hope (1 Thess. 4:13). Even in our crying, there can be an underlying joy, because we know death is not the end of the story.

LOVE IN VIEW OF ETERNITY

That young man Jesus resurrected from the dead ended up dying again later on. Every person Jesus raised from the dead eventually died again. Jesus wasn't doing it as a permanent solution, but rather as a temporary blessing foreshadowing an eternal reality.

Jesus makes eternal love possible. I think we're all preprogrammed with a desire for love that extends beyond a lifetime. One of the most popular book and movie series in recent years deals with the concept of eternal love. It may not be the most obvious movie choice for a guy, but I went to see it because I love my wife and Ashley loves those movies. Sometimes we do crazy things for the ones we love.

Twilight follows a young woman named Bella who falls in love with a vampire who never ages or dies.

Bella has to choose between Edward the vampire and another good-looking guy named Jacob, who happens to be a werewolf. (Just as a quick bit of dating advice for any single ladies: If your only dating prospects are a vampire and a werewolf, it might be time for you to broaden your options. Set up an online dating profile or something. There are plenty of human guys out there.)

In the end, Bella chooses the vampire, and through a bizarre set of circumstances, she eventually becomes a vampire too. She and Edward live eternally ever after.

Apparently, the *Twilight* stories resonate with people, because they've grossed approximately a bagillion dollars so far. I still scratch my head when I think about it. Even though I may not understand the plotline, I definitely understand the desire for eternal love. It's a desire God put in our hearts, and it's a desire that he alone can fulfill.

Jesus died a physical death on the cross, but he didn't stay dead. Three days later, he rose from the grave, and Christians have been celebrating ever since. Jesus' resurrection wasn't merely a miracle; it was a promise of a future miracle for all of us. The reality of resurrection alters the way we live and the way we love.

OUR LIVES AND OUR LOVE ARE NOT CONFINED TO THE YEARS ON A TOMBSTONE BETWEEN BIRTH AND DEATH.

Jesus has made it possible for all of us to live forever. In him and through him, we all have that same promise of resurrection and eternal life. This means our lives and our love are not confined to the years on a tombstone between birth and death. A life of love has the power to shape eternity.

LOVE CAN'T FIT INTO A LIFETIME

My buddy Jamey is a police officer in Georgia, and yesterday he had to report to a home where a woman had just died of natural causes. As he made his way into the house, he saw a frail, elderly man weeping by the bed where his beloved wife lay. My friend was moved by the tenderness, devotion, and love that had obviously held this marriage together for so many years.

After the coroner came, Jamey had the opportunity to sit down with the grieving husband to hear some wonderful stories. A surge of youthful energy flooded the old man's voice as he described their teenage marriage and how they'd run off to the West Coast with only pennies in their pockets to start their new life together. The sparkle in his eyes was undeniable as he relived their lifetime of love and adventure.

He shared some of the good times and bad times and how their commitment to each other, their faith, and their family had kept them grounded through all the storms. Their friendship had grown throughout their lives as they became companions, confidants, and collaborators through every season of their epic journey. Even as their health faded, their love grew. They shared so much laughter and love, and even through the trials they made sure there was always joy and fun.

When it came time for Jamey to leave, the old man shared one last thought that will forever stick in my mind. He said, "Sixty-six years together . . . it wasn't nearly enough time. There was so much time I wasted that I wish I could go back and give to her and spend with her. It just wasn't nearly enough time together."

The lesson for all of us is to cherish our time. Even in the little, everyday routines of life, be fully present in the moments together. Be willing to turn off the phones and screens and distractions and make time for each other. At the end of your life looking back, your faith and your family will be all that matters, so please don't wait until then to make them your top priority. Your love will be the only part of your legacy that can last into eternity.

Make a deliberate decision right now to stop wasting time and start putting first things first. Give the very best of yourself to your loved ones, not the leftovers after you've given your best to everyone and everything else.

So many people wait until they're at the end of life before they discover what matters most. They enter into eternity having squandered their time on earth. That's a tragedy I want to help you avoid at all costs.

> LIFE IS SHORT, BUT ETERNITY IS LONG. MAKE THE MOST OF EVERY MOMENT YOU HAVE ON EARTH.

Life is short, but eternity is long. Make the most of every moment you have on earth.

"Teach us to number our days, that we may gain a heart of wisdom" (Ps. 90:12 NIV).

Here are some ways to make the most of every moment, so when that time comes, you can face it with no regrets:

1. Be quick to forgive and to seek forgiveness.

Life's too short to hold grudges and keep a tally of each other's faults. Let grace flow freely. It will lift a huge weight off your shoulders and theirs.

2. Don't take each other for granted.

Recognize that every minute together is a gift, so treasure it. Don't prioritize your hobby, your career, or your possessions over your marriage and family. In the end, your relationships will be all that matters, so don't wait to make them your priority.

3. Laugh more.

Don't take yourselves too seriously, but don't take your commitments too lightly. Live life with conviction and purpose, but make plenty of room for fun. Laughter should be the soundtrack of your relationships.

4. Don't hit the snooze button on your dreams.

If you and your family have dreams, don't keep putting them off until "someday" gets here, because someday may never come unless you make it happen.

5. Realize that most of the stuff you fight about isn't worth fighting over.

Fight for each other, but never fight against each other. In every disagreement, remember that your relationship is much more important than whatever you're arguing about.

6. Remember that romance has no expiration date.

So many marriages start out strong and then slowly fade until there's nothing left, but it isn't supposed to be that way. Through all the seasons of your life, continue to pursue each other, love each other, encourage each other, and treasure every moment together. If you've already fallen out of those habits, start today and begin again.

7. Realize that good-bye doesn't have to be the end.

Love was created to last forever. Jesus promises the hope of eternal life and eternal love. Because of him, "good-bye" is never the last word. That same hope can be yours, and I can tell you from experience, it changes everything.

TROPHIES WORTH KEEPING

I learned a lot of useful information during my years at college, but one of the most memorable lessons didn't come in a classroom. It wasn't taught by a professor or a textbook. In fact, the lesson came in the most unlikely of ways.

A few mischievous friends and I had tried to carry out a century-old tradition by climbing into the steeple of our chapel on the campus of Georgetown College. We got lost in that big, dark building, so we never actually made it to the steeple, but we did find something that would forever change my perspective.

Our misguided quest led us to a hidden door. We entered a dark room. Enough moonlight was trickling in through the old, stained-glass windows for us to see that the room was full of something. My curiosity got the best of me, and I decided that I had to flip the light switch to see where we were, even if it meant we got caught trespassing.

As my eyes began to adjust to the light and the room came into focus, it took me a moment to comprehend what I was seeing. From floor to ceiling, from wall to wall, this room was packed full of a hundred years' worth of . . . trophies. There were trophies for everything: music, academics, football, baseball, philanthropy, and everything else you can imagine.

These awards had once been raised in moments of celebration, but now they sat in a forgotten room. People had worked so hard to achieve these trophies. They represented accomplishment and sacrifice, but now they lay in broken pieces in dusty boxes. They didn't seem to matter at all.

A quote I'd heard from Dr. James Dobson rang in my ears: "Life will trash your trophies."

Standing in that forgotten room was a transformative experience for me. I decided I didn't want to spend my life chasing trophies that wouldn't really matter. I didn't want my life's achievements to be things that could be stuffed in a forgotten, dusty room.

Achievements and awards are nice, but the enduring treasures are our relationships. Our relationships must always trump our trophies. Trophies can't love us back.

Don't neglect your friends or your family in pursuit of wealth or success. Any success you achieve at the expense of your relationships isn't really success. Live your life so that when you reach the end, you'll be surrounded by loved ones.

ETERNAL PERSPECTIVE

God wants you to live in the moment. He wants you to savor every minute you have with your loved ones on this planet, but he also wants you to live with an eternal perspective. Realizing death isn't the end should change the way we live and the way we love.

REALIZING DEATH ISN'T THE END SHOULD CHANGE THE WAY WE LIVE AND THE WAY WE LOVE.

I was watching a football game recently on DVR. I knew the outcome of the game because I'd seen the final score on the news before I watched the replay. My team won! Knowing I already had the victory changed the entire experience of watching the game.

As I watched the game unfold, there were times my team was losing. I started thinking to myself, *Oh, no! We're behind! We won't be able to come back. This isn't going to end well.*

Then I would come to my senses and realize, *Wait! The end is already decided. Victory is certain. We've already won!*

When the opposition would score, it wasn't pleasant to watch, but I could smile because I knew the final outcome.

You and I are living lives full of ups and downs. There are days that seem like a victory, and other days we feel defeated. On

> LOVE ISN'T A STORY WITH A HAPPY ENDING. LOVE IS A STORY WITH *NO* ENDING!

the hard days it's easy to look around and become discouraged. It's easy to feel like things are never going to work out.

I want you to be reassured with the truth of God's eternal promises. The end of the story is already written, and we win! Jesus has claimed victory. Through faith in him, we can rest assured that he will set all things right and make all things new. We'll get to celebrate with him and with our loved ones forever.

Love isn't a story with a happy ending. Love is a story with *no* ending!

A NEW HEART

"I will give you a new heart and put a new spirit in you; I will remove from you your heart of stone and give you a heart of flesh" (Ezek. 36:26 NIV).

One of the central teachings of the Bible is that God wants an eternal relationship with us transcending our mortal limitations. This is made possible because God gives us a spiritual heart transplant. I grew up in church learning this kind of terminology, but it honestly never made sense until I heard this story:

In my hometown, there was a young man named Paul. I never knew Paul personally, but I was in the same grade as one of his younger sisters. One night, Paul's parents received the kind of phone call that every parent dreads: their son had been in a terrible car accident. They rushed to the hospital, and when they arrived, their worst fears were confirmed. Paul had been killed. In an instant, life as they knew it had ended.

In that moment of tragedy and devastating pain, Paul's parents were forced to make the very difficult decision of whether or not to donate their son's organs. They decided that he would have wanted to save lives through his death, so with broken hearts they signed the papers and began the process of grieving this unimaginable loss.

After some time had passed, they decided they wanted to visit every person who had received the lifesaving gift of one of Paul's organs. The hospital contacted the recipients, and each was eager to thank them in person. They set out on a road trip to meet these people whose lives had been changed through their son.

Each encounter was heartwarming. They met a woman who had received one of Paul's kidneys, and she hugged them and thanked them and said that she would see her children grow up because of their son's sacrifice. They met a man who had received their son's liver, and he hugged them and cried and talked about the new life that their son had given him. They waited to visit the man who had received their son's heart last.

As they pulled up the gravel drive, they saw him come out of his house to welcome them, and before the car had come to a complete stop, Paul's mom had flung open the car door and raced to him. He stood in bewilderment as she threw her arms around him and squeezed him so tightly that he could barely breathe. After a few moments of awkward silence, he tried to introduce himself, but she immediately stopped him and said, "Shhhh. Please don't speak."

She finally pulled away just far enough for him to see the tears streaming down her face. She smiled, and with a trembling voice she looked into his eyes and said, "When I hold you close to me, I can feel my son's heart beating inside of you."

One day, you and I are going to pass from this life into eternity just as Paul has done. In that moment, the money we made, the fame we achieved, and the outward success we gained will seem very insignificant. In that moment, I believe God will rush to meet you with an embrace. The arms that created the universe will wrap themselves around you, and all he will want to say to you and me in that moment will be this:

WHEN WE CHOOSE TO LOVE PEOPLE THE WAY JESUS LOVES PEOPLE, THE WORLD WILL CHANGE.

"When I hold you close to me, I can feel my son's heart, the heart of Jesus, a heart of love, beating inside of you!"

When we choose to love people the way Jesus loves people, the world will change. Don't treat others the way they treat you; treat others the way God treats you. Embrace the love of Jesus in your own life, and then model the example of Jesus in your relationships. Jesus changed the world with love, and he wants you and me to continue in this. He wants to give you a new heart and a new life.

When you step from this life into eternity, love will be all that matters. Live your life with a heart of love. You'll be amazed at what will happen as a result.

DISCUSSION QUESTIONS

1. If you were faced with a terminal illness diagnosis today, what regrets would you have about your life? How can you start today and change those regrets?
2. How does your view of eternity shape your view of love?
3. How would you respond if someone threw a fake funeral surprise party for you?
4. What trophies are you tempted to value above relationships?
5. When you reach the end of your life, what would you like your legacy to be? What do you want your loved ones to say about you?

PART TWO

LOVE
IN ACTION

CHAPTER 8

LOVING YOUR SPOUSE

*So again I say, each man must love his wife as he loves
himself, and the wife must respect her husband.*

—EPHESIANS 5:33

My wife and I share a passion for helping people improve
their marriages. We have worked together to create many
marriage-building resources because we strongly believe that
when your marriage is strong, every other aspect of your life will
improve as a result. We don't claim to be experts, but we are honored to be encouragers for so many couples around the world.

It's hard to believe, but it's been almost fifteen years since I
asked Ashley to be my wife. I remember it like it was yesterday.

I had just returned home from a summer working at camp
before my senior year of college. Ashley and I had been talking
about marriage since our third date, and the time had come to
get the ring and plan a perfect evening. I wanted to close the
deal fast before she realized she was way out of my league and
could probably find a much better guy if she looked around.

With the help of her parents, I planned an elaborate story to give me an excuse to go and do some prep work. I told her that I needed to go visit my brother, who had just broken his collarbone. I hadn't thought through my backstory very well, because she said she wanted to come with me. So in a panic, I blurted out, "You can't . . . he's naked!"

"What? Why is he naked?"

"I don't know. When he's injured, he likes to be naked. I know, it's weird, but you can't come. He wouldn't want you to see him like that."

She was disappointed and confused when I left. I had knots in my stomach from nervousness and from the guilt of just having told her a ridiculous lie. To this day, I'm terrible at lying to her, which has actually worked out to be great for our marriage. After all, one of the Laws of Love is "Love Speaks Truth."

I finally made it back to take her to dinner, and everything was ready to go. She looked absolutely stunning in a red dress that brought out the beautiful tones of her strawberry-blonde hair. I kept thinking, *No way is she going to say yes. She is way out of my league!*

We went out to the nicest restaurant in town, and I paid a small fortune for a meal that I was too nervous to eat. Then we went to a place called Ashland, the estate of the famous Kentucky statesman, Henry Clay. The weather and the scenery were beautiful, but my hands were shaking as I pulled out a handwritten letter and began reading it to her. I professed my undying love and commitment and promised to always love and cherish her and to build our future on a foundation of faith in God. I got down on one knee and asked her to spend her life with me, and then she took a deep breath and exclaimed, "No way!"

My heart sank until I realized that it was a good "no way!" and she hugged me and said, "Yes!"

Four children and countless happy memories have been created since that awkward and beautiful moment nearly fifteen years ago. We've made a lot of mistakes along the way, but love and God's grace have held us together as we continue to learn on our journey.

Of all human relationships, God designed marriage to be the most powerful and intimate expression of love.

Even if you're not married, I believe this chapter can be helpful to you. God's plan for marriage mirrors the type of relationship God wants to have with each of us, so having a better understanding of marriage can ultimately help you have a clearer understanding of the God who created it.

> OF ALL HUMAN RELATIONSHIPS, GOD DESIGNED MARRIAGE TO BE THE MOST POWERFUL AND INTIMATE EXPRESSION OF LOVE.

THE POWER OF A NAKED MARRIAGE

One of the first love lessons we learned in our marriage was the power of a naked marriage. You probably think I'm just talking about sex right now, but there's a lot more to it than that. The sexual aspect of your marriage should be a huge priority, but remember that true intimacy requires more than just what happens in the bedroom. In the biblical book of Genesis, we're given the account of the first marriage. God created a couple who temporarily lived in an ideal setting with no debt, no crazy in-laws, no baggage, no stress, no fighting, and last but not least—no clothing!

"Now the man and his wife were both naked, but they felt no shame" (Gen. 2:25).

When God painted this picture of a naked marriage, I believe he was revealing to us something more than just sexual intimacy; he was revealing the importance of having complete transparency, vulnerability, acceptance, and intimacy at every level of the relationship. I'm certainly not advocating that we all walk around nude all day (although I do think most marriages would benefit from more naked time!), but I am suggesting that we all need to become more intentional about reconnecting with that true intimacy that Adam and Eve got a taste of in the garden of Eden.

Love in marriage.has to be completely open, honest, and transparent. Secrets are as dangerous as lies and can rob your relationship of intimacy and trust.

Love, by its very nature, is honest, and this is especially important to the sacred bond of trust in marriage. When you're not living in a naked marriage the way God intended, you're opening yourself up to very dangerous temptations. Those temptations have led many down a dark path. My friend Jesse is a dramatic example of this.

Jesse had finally hit rock bottom. While his wife was out of town, he found himself sitting at a computer screen late one evening to solicit anonymous sex. His porn habit had evolved into a full-blown addiction and ultimately had created a devastating pattern of depravity and self-destructive behavior.

His life was out of control, and his marriage was in shambles. He was completely miserable, but he felt powerless to change the situation. As he sat in that dark room planning dark deeds, he caught a glimpse of his reflection from the computer screen and realized that he no longer recognized the man he had become.

That night some light broke through the darkness, and Jesse

finally realized that he needed to take immediate action to set things right. He called out to God for help, and he made a commitment to do everything in his power to break free from sexual sin and to rebuild his wife's trust. He set out on a long journey to reclaim his honor and his family.

Several years have passed, and I'm happy to say that Jesse and his wife, Tricia, are happier than they have ever been in their marriage. He has an amazing wife, two beautiful sons, a successful career in the US military, and many great adventures ahead. Today, as I'm writing these words, they are on a plane to Germany, where they will spend the next three years. I spoke with him on the phone two days ago, and his voice was filled with excitement and anticipation as he talked and dreamed about the great days ahead.

You might be reading all this and wondering how it's possible for a marriage to be restored after that kind of behavior. It happened because of a tremendous amount of grace from God and from Jesse's wife. Grace alone was only part of the equation. This marriage was saved because Jesse was willing to put some uncompromising boundaries in place. Those boundaries created a protected climate where trust could be rebuilt and healing could begin.

He recognized that he had become powerless to fight the battles by willpower alone, so he surrounded himself with people who could encourage him and keep him accountable. He started a support group for men who were wrestling with similar struggles, and that group provided an outlet for continued growth and healing. Together, those men talked, prayed, laughed, cried, studied the Bible, and found practical solutions to the issues that haunted them.

Jesse's newfound boundaries also included putting a filter

on his computer that tracked and documented every website that he visited and giving his wife complete access to that information. He also gave his wife full access to his phone, texts, voice mails, e-mails, and all of his communication devices. He then cut off all contact with certain "friends" and committed to never return to places that could put him in tempting or compromising situations. Those boundaries created a framework where his marriage could be rebuilt.

> IF YOUR MARRIAGE SEEMS LIKE IT'S STUCK IN A RUT, ONE REASON MAY BE SECRETS THAT NEED TO COME OUT INTO THE OPEN.

If your marriage seems like it's stuck in a rut, one reason may be secrets that need to come out into the open. When those secrets bring pain or broken trust, remember the Law that "Love Offers Grace." It may take time to fully trust again, but forgiveness should come instantly. You'll be amazed at the power of honesty and grace. Don't keep score of each other's faults, but extend grace the way God has freely given grace to us. Forgiveness will always lead to healing, but holding grudges will always create unnecessary pain. Consider this timeless truth from the Bible's book of wisdom: "Love prospers when a fault is forgiven, but dwelling on it separates close friends" (Prov. 17:9). Let truth and forgiveness flow freely in your marriage, and you'll be able to get through any challenge that comes your way.

ONE OF THE MOST COMMON MISTAKES IN MARRIAGE

We tend to think that all marriage problems stem from a big breach of trust like the one in the story I just shared, but some can be caused by something completely different. Very often, the lack of love isn't because of a one-time sin but an ongoing pattern of behavior leading to what I call a cable-company marriage. I know that probably sounds pretty random, so let me explain.

Have you ever noticed how cable companies treat their customers with amazing care and attentiveness when they're first trying to seal the deal, but once they've got you, the introductory rates are replaced with much more expensive rates and the customer service takes a nosedive, which makes you want to trade in your old cable company for a new one? The cable TV industry seems focused on a model of treating people really well at first but then taking them for granted in the long run.

Sadly, a lot of marriages operate this way too. In the beginning, when the couple is trying to win each other's hearts, they roll out the red carpet. They give the very best of themselves, but it doesn't last long. Once the day-to-day reality of life together sets in, they stop doing all those things they did in the beginning. They take each other for granted, and it isn't long before they both start longing for something new where they'll be treated well again.

It doesn't have to be this way! Marriages should grow stronger with time. Couples should continue pursuing, encouraging, and adoring each other through all the seasons of the relationship.

If you find yourself in a cable-company marriage right now, don't lose hope. Don't throw away your relationship just to start anew with someone else and repeat the same cycle. Make a commitment to transform your marriage. Stop taking each other for granted. Your best days together can still be ahead of you and not behind you.

One of the most effective ways to break out of a rut in your marriage is to selflessly serve. One of the last lessons Jesus taught his disciples on earth was to serve one another. He gave them a practical example by washing their feet, one after the other, following their final meal together.

ONE OF THE MOST EFFECTIVE WAYS TO BREAK OUT OF A RUT IN YOUR MARRIAGE IS TO SELFLESSLY SERVE.

Serving creates an antidote to the toxicity of complacency in marriage. When a couple chooses to serve each other and also chooses to serve others together, the marriage instantly improves. I watched a video recently about a couple named Francis and Lisa Chan, who put this concept into practice in a beautiful and unique way. Francis Chan is a pastor and bestselling author. I've been an admirer of his work for a long time, but I was still blown away by what he did to celebrate his twentieth wedding anniversary.

The Chans wanted to do something special to mark two decades of marriage. They looked into resorts around the globe, but then they decided to do something completely unconventional. Instead of going someplace where they could be served, they wanted to go someplace where they could serve others.

They bought two plane tickets to Africa and went to visit some missionaries they had been financially supporting. Francis and Lisa rolled up their sleeves and served food to hungry people, constructed shelters for homeless people, and worked alongside their missionary friends to free women who were trapped in a cycle of poverty and prostitution.

The couple had tears in their eyes as they shared this experience. It became one of the most extraordinary experiences of their lives. They came home from their life-changing anniversary trip and decided to write a book together, putting their hearts on paper in *You and Me Forever: Marriage in Light of Eternity*.

Every penny made from the sale of their book is being donated to the ministries in Africa where they served together for their twentieth anniversary.

When you and your spouse reach the end of your time on earth, what will matter most will be the moments you served each other and the moments you served alongside each other. When we remove selfishness from our marriages, love will be all that remains. That's the kind of love that can change your marriage and change the world through your marriage.

> ANY RELATIONSHIP LEFT ON AUTOPILOT WILL SLOWLY DRIFT TOWARD ATROPHY, BUT ANY RELATIONSHIP GIVEN CONSISTENT INVESTMENTS OF TIME, FOCUS, AND SELFLESS SERVICE WILL FLOURISH UNTIL THE END.

Wherever you are in your relationship, know that you can grow stronger. Any relationship left on autopilot will slowly drift toward atrophy, but any relationship given consistent investments of time, focus, and selfless service will flourish until the end.

IN SICKNESS AND IN HEALTH

My friends Freddy and Linda have a remarkable marriage, but you wouldn't know just how remarkable by looking at the surface. On Freddy's skull, there are some deep scars. Those scars tell a story of redemption, love, and the power of a wife who made a vow to love her husband in sickness and in health and really meant it.

Several years back, Freddy suffered a traumatic brain injury that rendered him nearly incapacitated. He couldn't speak, and he could do nothing for himself. For over a year, Linda was his sole caregiver. She loved and cared for him with a tenderhearted compassion that melted the hearts of all who saw them together. It was a difficult time for her, but her commitment to him was unshakable.

After a year of round-the-clock caregiving, the impossible happened. If you don't believe in modern-day miracles, it's probably because you haven't met Freddy. Against all odds and doctors' dire predictions, Freddy began to emerge from his catatonic state and regain his mental and physical capacity.

Today, Freddy is as sharp as ever, and he and Linda are some of the most faithful leaders in our church. Freddy, who was helpless a few short years ago, is now able to serve and support Linda through a challenging season in her own life. Their partnership, faith, and commitment to each other is a wonderful picture of what marriage can and should be.

I'm not sure what terminology the doctors used to make sense of Freddy's remarkable recovery. There are probably some big, fancy, scientific terms used to demystify the miracle. For me, I think it's all a result of love. Freddy is a walking miracle and a testament to love's healing power.

My wife has a beautiful saying that always makes me think of Freddy and Linda. Ashley says, "A strong marriage rarely has two strong people at the same time. It is a husband and wife who take turns being strong for each other in the moments when the other feels weak."

THE "PERFECT" HUSBAND: MAN'S VIEW VERSUS GOD'S VIEW

God's definition of a healthy marriage is often different from what we see in the world around us. I believe one of the most important first steps in preparing to be a husband or wife is to develop a clear understanding of what being a good husband or good wife really means. The reality is often something different from what we see in culture.

When billionaire Donald Trump married a supermodel who was less than half his age, a talk show host who was interviewing the new Mrs. Trump asked the question that everyone else was thinking: "Would you have married him if he wasn't rich?"

She smiled and gave an unexpected reply: "Would he have married me if I wasn't beautiful?"

We all have in our minds what a perfect spouse looks like, and it is often a picture we get from the world's superficial value system rather than from God. The Bible says that people tend to look at the outward appearance, but God looks at the heart. He doesn't measure the worth of a husband or wife by how much money he might have in the bank or by how much she weighs. It's an issue of the heart, and he has given us a clear path to follow.

For husbands, our role model is Jesus. You might be thinking, *Wait a minute. I didn't think Jesus was ever even married?*

Yes, you're right, but Jesus is often referred to as the bridegroom,

> WE ALL HAVE IN OUR MINDS WHAT A PERFECT SPOUSE LOOKS LIKE, AND IT IS OFTEN A PICTURE WE GET FROM THE WORLD'S SUPERFICIAL VALUE SYSTEM RATHER THAN FROM GOD.

and husbands are called to imitate the relationship Jesus has with his bride, the church. Based on that example, here are a few key roles that every husband must strive to fill each and every day:

A husband loves his wife passionately and selflessly.

Jesus was the embodiment of love, and he showed us that love is much more about action and commitment than it is about feeling. He pursued us passionately and then displayed the ultimate love by dying in our place on the cross. The Bible specifically calls husbands to love their wives with that same type of selfless love.

> "For husbands, this means love your wives, just as Christ loved the church. He gave up his life for her" (Eph. 5:25).

A husband serves his wife.

Jesus was a king, but he laid down his rights to be served and instead served others. As husbands, we are called to serve our wives and families. In practical terms, this means placing their needs ahead of our wants. It means prioritizing them ahead of our hobbies or even our careers. It means being willing to do dishes, fold laundry, or whatever else is needed to support our families.

> "But among you it will be different. Whoever wants to be a leader among you must be your servant, and whoever wants to be first among you must become your slave. For even the Son of Man came not to be served but to serve others and to give his life as a ransom for many" (Matt. 20:26–28).

A husband protects his wife.

Jesus was described as a shepherd. In his culture, a shepherd was one who would protect the sheep from any form of attack, even if it meant risking his own life in the process. As husbands, we are called to be the protectors of our wives and children. God gave you those manly muscles for a reason.

Physical protection is one part of the equation, but husbands need to be emotional and spiritual protectors as well. This means speaking words of encouragement and hope instead of belittlement or demand. It also means accepting God's call to lead our families into deeper spiritual maturity.

> "Don't be afraid of the enemy! Remember the Lord, who is great and glorious, and fight for your brothers, your sons, your daughters, your wives, and your homes!" (Neh. 4:14).

A husband provides for his wife.

Jesus provides every need both great and small. He set the example of the husband as provider by giving sight to a blind man, giving food to the hungry masses that hadn't eaten lunch, providing wine at a wedding banquet, and even giving his own life to bring salvation.

Providing financially is one part of this, but don't use that as an excuse to work so much that you are absent from your family. The greatest gift Jesus provided was himself, and the greatest gift you can provide is the gift of yourself. Part of providing means simply providing your own presence. Your wife and family can do with less of almost anything if it means having more of you.

"Work brings profit, but mere talk leads to poverty!"
(Prov. 14:23).

A husband communicates openly and honestly with his wife.

Most frustrations in marriage come either directly or indirectly from a breakdown in communication between husband and wife. Men and women both contribute in different ways. For men, the breakdown often comes through a lack of communication.

Our wives need for us to talk to them, and not just the way we talk about the weather or football with our guy friends. They need us to share the details of our day and listen carefully to what they are trying to communicate to us. Speak with truth and love, and listen with respect and compassion. If you'll make communication a priority, I believe every other aspect of your marriage will begin to improve.

> "Now you are my friends, since I have told you everything the Father told me" (John 15:15b).

THE "PERFECT" WIFE: MAN'S VIEW VERSUS GOD'S VIEW

Jesus is the standard-bearer for life and relationships for both husbands and wives. His example of selfless service, honesty, and love is equally applicable to the lives of men and women and should be followed by us all. The Bible has countless lessons for marriage, but the one passage most specifically focused on godly womanhood in the home is found in chapter 31 of the book of Proverbs. It gives us a snapshot of God's definition of a wife of noble character.

I'm truly thankful for the character of my wife, Ashley. I can honestly say that she embodies these traits better than anyone I know, and she inspires me to be the best husband, father, and man I can be. Next to God's grace, she is the greatest gift in my life. Strive to be that kind of blessing to your husband, and your marriage will thrive.

1. A wife brings respect to her husband.

Notice that she doesn't just give respect, but she actually brings respect. Your words and actions toward him actually have the power to either build him up or tear him down. Proverbs paints a picture of a man being more respected and more respectable because of the honor his wife has brought to him. Be the kind of wife who brings honor and respect to your husband and your family because of the investment you have made in their lives.

"Her husband is well known at the city gates, where he sits with the other civic leaders" (Prov. 31:23).

2. A wife provides a warm atmosphere in the home for her husband.

A wife of noble character will make it her mission to have a home full of peace and joy. There will always be moments of chaos along the way, because that's just how life works, but strive to create a life-giving environment. The wife is the heart of

THE WIFE IS THE HEART OF THE HOME, AND SHE IS THE PERSON MOST CAPABLE OF CREATING THE MOOD AND CLIMATE IN THE HOME.

the home, and she is the person most capable of creating the mood and climate in the home. So create a good one!

I am so thankful for the atmosphere that Ashley has created in our home. Her warmth, kind spirit, and eye for interior design have created a beautiful oasis for our children and for me. No matter how stressful a day I've had, when I walk through the door, I feel peace, and she is the reason why.

> "She is clothed with strength and dignity, and she laughs without fear of the future. When she speaks, her words are wise, and she gives instructions with kindness. She carefully watches everything in her household and suffers nothing from laziness" (Prov. 31:25–27).

3. A wife works hard to support her husband.

Some wives work in profitable careers outside the home, and some focus their work exclusively inside the home. In either situation, a wife should support her husband and family through diligence, resourcefulness, and hard work.

> "She gets up before dawn to prepare breakfast for her household and plan the day's work for her servant girls. She goes to inspect a field and buys it; with her earnings she plants a vineyard. She is energetic and strong, a hard worker. She makes sure her dealings are profitable; her lamp burns late into the night" (Prov. 31:15–18).

4. A wife looks her best for her husband.

While outward appearance isn't everything, a wife must realize that God created men to be visual creatures, and you honor your husband and your marriage when you strive to look your best. It will also increase your own confidence, health, and well-being.

> "She dresses in fine linen and purple gowns" (Prov. 31:22b).

5. A wife provides companionship for her husband.

One of the most important roles for a wife is simply to be a best friend to her husband. He desires your companionship. Create opportunities for the two of you to share new adventures and new experiences. As you grow in your friendship with each other, you'll also be growing in your love for each other. At the core of every healthy marriage is a healthy friendship.

> "Her husband can trust her, and she will greatly enrich his life. She brings him good, not harm, all the days of her life" (Prov. 31:11–12).

TWENTY-ONE DATE-NIGHT QUESTIONS

As we approach the end of this chapter, I want to give you a fun and interactive exercise. Just when you think you've come to know all there is to know about someone, you'll find out that you're just getting started. Marriage is a lifelong journey of discovery and communication. It is the only way to continue growing in your discovery of each other. To do this, you must make continuing conversation a priority.

MARRIAGE IS A LIFELONG JOURNEY OF DISCOVERY AND COMMUNICATION.

Below are some questions that should start some great

conversations. Turn off your phones and TV, and ask your spouse these questions. I guarantee that you'll both end up discovering something new and also have fun in the process.

1. If there was a movie about your life, what songs would you want on the soundtrack?
2. In that movie, what actor or actress (past or present) would you want to play you?
3. If you could have named yourself, what name would you have chosen?
4. What is your favorite quality about yourself?
5. What is one thing you wish you could change about yourself?
6. What was your biggest fear when you were a child?
7. What is your biggest fear now?
8. Besides our wedding and the day our kids were born, what is your all-time favorite day?
9. What would you do with the money if we won the lottery?
10. What would you do tomorrow if you lost your job and money and we had to start over?
11. When you were a kid, who was your biggest hero?
12. Who is your biggest hero today?
13. What is your greatest regret?
14. What is one thing you'd like to accomplish by this time next year?
15. If you won a free vacation to any place on earth, where would you want to go?
16. What was your first nickname?
17. What is your earliest childhood memory?
18. What was the moment when you laughed harder than you've ever laughed?

19. If you could write one new law that everyone had to obey, what law would you create?
20. What new hobby would you like to try?
21. Besides marrying me, what's the greatest thing that has ever happened to you?

THE BEST MARRIAGE ADVICE EVER

When Ashley and I got married thirteen years ago, we were young and in love, but we were also pretty clueless (me especially). Along the way, we've had so many people share wise advice and life experiences with us, which has helped guide our family through good times and hard times. Through the years, I've been collecting some of the best wisdom others have shared with us (and some I had to learn through my own mistakes).

As we wrap up this chapter, I want you to have the most practical and concise nuggets of marriage wisdom I've come across. If you'll apply the following twenty-five principles to your relationship, it could make a life-changing difference in your marriage. Some of these principles have been previously stated in the book, but I've collected them here for quick reference when you need a jolt of encouragement and advice. (In no particular order):

1. Choose to love each other even in those moments when you struggle to like each other. Love is a commitment, not a feeling.
2. Always answer the phone when your husband/wife is calling and, when possible, try to keep your phone off when you're together with your spouse.

3. Make time together a priority. Budget for a consistent date night. Time is the currency of relationships, so consistently invest time in your marriage.

4. Surround yourself with friends who will strengthen your marriage, and remove yourself from people who may tempt you to compromise your character.

5. Make laughter the soundtrack of your marriage. Share moments of joy, and even in the hard times find reasons to laugh.

6. In every argument, remember that there won't be a winner and a loser. You are partners in everything, so you'll either win together or lose together. Work together to find a solution.

7. Remember that a strong marriage rarely has two strong people at the same time. It's usually a husband and wife taking turns being strong for each other in the moments when the other feels weak.

8. Prioritize what happens in the bedroom. It takes more than sex to build a strong marriage, but it's nearly impossible to build a strong marriage without it.

9. Remember that marriage isn't 50–50; divorce is 50–50. Marriage has to be 100–100. It's not splitting everything in half but both partners giving everything they've got.

10. Give your best to each other, not your leftovers after you've given your best to everyone else.

11. Learn from other people, but don't feel the need to compare your life or your marriage to anyone else's. God's plan for your life is masterfully unique.

12. Don't put your marriage on hold while you're raising your kids, or else you'll end up with an empty nest and an empty marriage.

13. Never keep secrets from each other. Secrecy is the enemy of intimacy.

14. Never lie to each other. Lies break trust, and trust is the foundation of a strong marriage.

15. When you've made a mistake, admit it and humbly seek forgiveness. You should be quick to say, "I was wrong. I'm sorry. Please forgive me."

16. When your husband/wife breaks your trust, give them your forgiveness instantly, which will promote healing and create the opportunity for trust to be rebuilt. You should be quick to say, "I love you. I forgive you. Let's move forward."

17. Be patient with each other. Your spouse is always more important than your schedule.

18. Model the kind of marriage that will make your sons want to grow up to be good husbands and your daughters want to grow up to be good wives.

19. Be your spouse's biggest encourager, not his/her biggest critic. Be the one who wipes away your spouse's tears, not the one who causes them.

20. Never talk badly about your spouse to other people or vent about them online. Protect your spouse at all times and in all places.

21. Always wear your wedding ring. It will remind you that you're always connected to your spouse, and it will remind the rest of the world that you're off limits.

22. Connect with a community of faith. A good church can make a world of difference in your marriage and family.

23. Pray together. Every marriage is stronger with God in the middle of it.

24. When you have to choose between saying nothing or

saying something mean to your spouse, say nothing every time.

25. Never consider divorce as an option. Remember that a perfect marriage is just two imperfect people who refuse to give up on each other.

FINAL THOUGHTS

We're often guilty of showing more respect and thoughtfulness to strangers and coworkers throughout our day than we show to our spouses. There is no human relationship more sacred than our marriages, so treasure your spouse. The more you love your spouse, the more capacity you will have to love everyone else. Never let anyone or anything take the place of priority your spouse should hold in your heart.

DISCUSSION QUESTIONS

1. What is one thing you learned from watching your parents' marriage?
2. Who is a couple in your life who seems to have a rock-solid marriage, and what is it about their relationship that makes them so strong?
3. What do you think are the factors that separate healthy couples from unhealthy couples?
4. What are some of the goals you have for your marriage (or your future marriage)?

CHAPTER 9

LOVING YOUR FAMILY

Love each other with genuine affection, and take delight
in honoring each other.

—ROMANS 12:10

A shley was a refined, classy, lovely woman who grew up in a house full of girls. By contrast, I was basically a caveman who had been raised in a house full of guys. Our family backgrounds were very different, which required a big adjustment for us both.

For instance, I never use clippers on my toenails. This is something she discovered after we were married. It didn't seem weird to me. I always thought, *Why would you want to take something sharp and put it on your toes?*

When my toenails start getting too long, I just pick at them, leaving sharp, jagged edges. I am like Wolverine, except the claws grow out of my feet. I know what you're thinking, and you're right. It's a disgusting habit.

One night, we were sound asleep. Around 2:00 A.M., I woke

up to the sound of Ashley screaming out in pain. I was terrified; I was confused. I was stumbling around, thinking there was an intruder in the house. It was pure chaos!

We turned the lights on, and her leg was bleeding. I thought someone had broken into our house and stabbed my beautiful wife in the leg. In our delusional state, we started trying to piece together all the evidence, and we realized there was some blood on my big toe as well. We finally deciphered the clues and solved the mystery. I was the intruder, and my disgusting toenail was the weapon!

Looking back on that crazy night brings a lot of laughter, but it also raises some important questions. If we're supposed to love and cherish our families, how do we do it in spite of all their unlovable flaws? Does love make us ignore, accept, or attempt to change one another's imperfections?

LOVE AND FAMILY

When God created the concept of a family, he simultaneously gave us an extraordinary gift and an extraordinary challenge. Family requires an unshakable commitment to one another even when everyone involved is intimately aware of one another's flaws.

> FAMILY REQUIRES AN UNSHAKABLE COMMITMENT TO ONE ANOTHER EVEN WHEN EVERYONE INVOLVED IS INTIMATELY AWARE OF ONE ANOTHER'S FLAWS.

These iconic words are from "The Love Chapter" found in the Bible.

Love is patient and kind. Love is not jealous or boastful or proud or rude. It does not demand its own way. It is not irritable, and it keeps no record of being wronged. It does not rejoice about injustice but rejoices whenever the truth wins out. Love never gives up, never loses faith, is always hopeful, and endures through every circumstance (1 Cor. 13:4–7).

First Corinthians 13 contains some of the most famous words ever written about love. These famous words aren't just a poetic description of love; they also represent a very practical road map to guide your family in the right direction.

Let's take a moment to briefly unpack these verses and explore what their application might look like in your family:

- Love is patient and kind, so be patient and kind with one another.
- Love is not boastful or proud, so refuse to allow the poison of pride to taint your relationships.
- Love is not self-seeking, so choose to put your family's needs ahead of your own.
- Love is not easily angered, so allow no place for spite or hostility in your home.
- Love keeps no record of wrongs, so allow grace and forgiveness to flow freely.
- Love rejoices with the truth, so refuse to deceive or keep secrets from one another.
- Love always protects and perseveres, so never give up on one another.

Make a conscious decision to love one another using God's definition of love. Allow your family to be led by love, and you'll always be headed in the right direction.

THE FAMILY OF GOD

Family is one of God's greatest gifts. Of course, all of us have a few rowdy relatives we'd probably never choose to hang out with if we weren't related, but even with the occasionally awkward Thanksgiving dinner, most of us can agree that family is a wonderful blessing. A family is masterfully designed to provide support, encouragement, accountability, love, and a place to call home. It fills the most crucial human needs.

> **GOD'S ULTIMATE PLAN FOR FAMILY REACHES BEYOND JUST THE PHYSICAL INTO THE SPIRITUAL.**

God's ultimate plan for family reaches beyond just the physical into the spiritual. He has created a family that will last forever, and the Bible has a lot to say about how it looks and how we can and should be a part of it. Here are a few truths the Bible teaches on the subject of God's family:

1. God intended his church to be a family.

In God's design, family extends beyond biological relatives. The church is not a building or an organization. It's a body of believers making up a family. The world attempts to define us by race, gender, age, socioeconomic status, outward appearance, and all kinds of other factors that don't really define who we are, but the church is a place where all those labels should disappear and be replaced by the unity we have in Christ.

> "There is no longer Jew or Gentile, slave or free, male and female. For you are all one in Christ Jesus" (Gal. 3:28).

2. As a family, we are defined by our love.

Jesus never intended for his followers to be identified by how they look or by the bumper stickers on their cars. The DNA of God's family is simply love. We must have a love for God and for one another. That's how the world will know we're part of God's family.

> "Your love for one another will prove to the world that you are my disciples" (John 13:35).

3. As a family, we need to take care of one another.

God designed the church so that every person in it would have his or her needs met. Financially, relationally, and emotionally, we need to support one another and work together to provide hope and healing to people outside the church as well.

> "Therefore, whenever we have the opportunity, we should do good to everyone—especially to those in the family of faith" (Gal. 6:10).

4. God wants you in his family.

Maybe you feel like you don't belong anywhere, but you were created to be part of God's family. It begins by reaching out to Jesus in faith.

> "Anyone who does the will of my Father in heaven is my brother and sister and mother!" (Matt. 12:50).

LOVE AND PARENTING

The concepts of love we've been learning thus far apply to every familial relationship, whether it's among a church family, siblings, parents, children, or in-laws. For the remainder of this chapter, I'm going to focus primarily on the role of love in the context of parenting, simply because it's where we tend to need practical principles the most. It also represents a generational impact. Your parenting won't just affect your kids, but it will shape future generations of your family.

I don't know about you, but most days I feel completely unqualified to be a parent. The life, health, training, and livelihood of four little boys is a huge responsibility, and most days I feel like I fall way short. I recognize that God has given my wife and me the privilege of raising Cooper, Connor, Chandler, and Chatham, and I want to raise them to be strong, courageous, faithful, smart, thoughtful, respectful, and wise men of character. I often feel like I can't compete with the world's bombardment of negative influences. If you're a parent, you can probably relate to my feelings of inadequacy.

I recently heard a preacher named Mike Breaux tell the story of being outside on a warm, Kentucky summer night and noticing the lights in the sky. He noticed the moon and the stars and the lights from a distant factory down the road, but then all of those big lights were eclipsed by a new light that captured his full attention. A lightning bug lit up right by his face, and that little firefly was all he could see.

> "YOU CAN IMPRESS PEOPLE FROM A DISTANCE, BUT YOU CAN ONLY IMPACT THEM FROM UP CLOSE!"

In that moment he realized that there are all kinds of lights (outside influences) competing for the attention of his kids, and if he wanted to be the biggest influence in his kids' lives, he didn't have to be the biggest or the brightest. He just had to be the closest! That beautifully simple word picture stuck in my mind and revealed the secret for having (and continuing to have) the most impact on my children.

It's the same for all of us. Howard Hendricks has wisely stated, "You can impress people from a distance, but you can only impact them from up close!"

There will always be impressive-looking forces trying to be the primary influence on our kids, but we can make the biggest impact by simply staying close to our sons and daughters. Make quality (and quantity) time with them a priority. Refuse to let outside influences pull them in the wrong direction. Give them a solid foundation of faith and love, and know that even though we are all imperfect parents, we have a perfect heavenly Father who is by our side through it all.

Seven Ways Parents Harm Their Children Without Even Realizing It

As a parent, I blow it pretty much every day in some way. Sometimes it's when I lose my temper and yell at the kids. Other times, it's when I burp out loud at the dinner table right after I've scolded one of my boys for doing the same thing.

With most of my parenting blunders, I'm instantly aware of the mistake, which gives me the opportunity to apologize and try to correct it. But I've found that some of the most dangerous parenting mistakes aren't obvious. They're subtle and stealthy. This makes them even more dangerous, because we can go on doing them for years without even realizing we're harming our kids in the process.

As I have worked with families from all walks of life, I'm convinced that the list below represents some of the most common and destructive parenting mistakes. I'm not writing this as an expert but just as a dad who is in the trenches and is desperately trying to get this right for the sake of my kids and future generations of my family.

If you're a parent too, let's commit to stopping these behaviors and being the best we can be for our kids.

1. Subtle dishonesty

Kids are human lie detectors, and we can't teach them the value of honesty and integrity when we're willing to be dishonest. We can't cheat on our taxes and still have the moral authority to teach our kids they shouldn't cheat in school. We need to teach our kids to tell the truth even when it's inconvenient or costly.

2. Emotional sabotage

It's easy to fly off the handle when our children aren't listening or when they're being careless or disobedient. Sometimes we'll even use our emotions just to get a reaction from our kids. This is dangerous, because when we can't control our emotional reactions to our children, we're teaching them that they are in control of our emotions instead of us. This can create a long-term pattern of emotional dysfunction in the home.

3. The comparison trap

In an attempt to encourage or correct our children, we might point out the example of another child (often a sibling) as a reference point. While this is usually a harmless attempt to bring context to the situation, most children won't see past the comparison. This can subconsciously train children not to be the best they can be, but rather to find a way to simply seem better than their peers and siblings.

4. Guilty gifts

In our culture (I'm writing from an American perspective), we've developed a bad habit of buying our kids' affection with gifts. When we've made a mistake or had to work late, we're much more likely to repay the relational debt with money. This cycle can teach our kids to be materialistic and to see love as a transactional relationship that can be manipulated by money. We all know (or should know) that real love is something much more valuable than that.

5. Putting the happiness of your children ahead of the health of your marriage

Many couples won't even go on a date night because they're afraid the children will cry. To pacify the kids, they never invest in their relationship with each other. Ironically, many of these kids end up crying anyway after divorce rips the family in two. One of the greatest gifts you can give your children is the security that comes from seeing their parents in a loving, committed marriage.

6. Digital babysitters

I've been guilty of this one a lot. In our technology-driven world, it's easy to plop the kids down in front of a screen so we can get some stuff done. In small doses, this is okay, but it can develop into a dangerous habit where we're delegating our most sacred duty of raising our kids to TV shows and video games.

7. Hiding your flaws

We all want our kids to see us as superheroes who never make mistakes, but our kids aren't looking for perfection. They're looking for authenticity. When you've blown it, own it! Use it as a teaching moment. Remember that God is the only perfect parent, and his grace has got you covered in those moments when you mess up (and we all have plenty of those).

Seven Values All Parents Must Teach Their Kids

Loving our kids requires more than just avoiding negative mistakes; it means proactively and consistently teaching them the values that matter most.

After looking at everything the Bible (the world's greatest

parenting manual) has to say about parenthood and borrowing wisdom from some parents who are much wiser than I am, I've put together a list of the seven most important lessons all parents must teach their children. If you consistently teach these values, you'll be raising future world-changers!

Take responsibility for teaching these lessons to your kids. It's not the government's job, it's not the schoolteacher's job, and it's not even the church's job. You can't delegate the responsibility of parenting. God entrusted these kids to *you*. It's your great privilege and your sacred duty to impart these timeless values to your children.

> YOU CAN'T DELEGATE THE RESPONSIBILITY OF PARENTING.

1. Tell the truth.

"I could have no greater joy than to hear that my children are following the truth" (3 John v. 4).

2. Honor your parents.

"Honor your father and mother. Then you will live a long, full life in the land the LORD your God is giving you" (Ex. 20:12).

3. Love one another.

"Dear children, let's not merely say that we love each other; let us show the truth by our actions" (1 John 3:18).

4. Do your best.

"Work willingly at whatever you do, as though you

were working for the Lord rather than for people" (Col. 3:23).

5. Be patient.

"Always be humble and gentle. Be patient with each other, making allowance for each other's faults because of your love" (Eph. 4:2).

6. Be thankful.

"Be thankful in all circumstances, for this is God's will for you who belong to Christ Jesus" (1 Thess. 5:18).

7. Never give up.

"I have fought the good fight, I have finished the race, and I have remained faithful" (2 Tim. 4:7).

MY FAVORITE PARENTING ADVICE

I want this chapter to be as practical as possible, so I'm including some of my all-time favorite parenting advice. These nuggets of wisdom have helped me love and lead my kids with more focus, and I hope these tips do the same for you:

1. Don't use anger to get action. Use action to get action.

Dr. James Dobson taught this basic principle, which has deeply resonated with me. As parents, we all fight the temptation to respond to our children's disobedience with anger, but anger doesn't work. Action does. When we calmly respond by giving cool-headed discipline, then our kids will also respond. Granted, this is easier said than done, but it really does work.

2. Be intentional about what you reward.

Discipline isn't just handing out negative consequences; it is also rewarding positive behavior. Sometimes we inadvertently reward negative behavior by giving in to our kids' demands because we're tired of fighting about it. This is a huge mistake because we're actually reinforcing their negative behavior when we do that. One principle I've found to be so true is that rewarded behavior is repeated behavior.

3. Give clear boundaries.

In a football game, every player on the field knows what is out of bounds. On the highway, every driver knows not to cross the double yellow lines. Those boundaries are there for the protection of all, and they actually exist to give freedom, not to restrict it. Many times our kids don't have any idea what behavior is out of bounds because we constantly change the rules based on our own emotions. We've got to clearly and consistently communicate the boundaries. Doing so will give our kids confidence and the ability to succeed.

4. Give unconditional love *and* high expectations.

Most of us are good at either giving our kids a lot of love and encouragement *or* giving them a lot of correction. We either come across like a Hallmark card or like a drill sergeant. Kids are complex, and they actually need *both*.

A LETTER TO MY KIDS

As I close this chapter, I want to share a letter to my kids. If you have children, I encourage you to write your own letter to them. Your words have the power to shape their view of love and their view of themselves.

Cooper, Connor, Chandler, and Chatham,

You guys are too young to care anything about reading Dad's book right now, but one day, I hope you stumble across this and get something out of it. Above everything else I write, always know that you are loved. You are each a gift from God, and your mom and I are so blessed to be your parents.

Remember that the measure of a man has nothing to do with your stature, your salary, or your success; it's a matter of the heart. Being a man means taking responsibility. It means protecting the weak, defending the truth, providing for those under your care, selflessly serving and loving your wife, providing a genuine example for your children, and leaving every person and place a little better off than you found them. This is the duty of every man.

> THE BIBLE IS YOUR ROAD MAP FOR LIFE, SO MAKE SURE YOU KNOW IT WELL.

Each of you will be a leader someday, but as you lead, remember that unless you love those you're leading, you're not worth following. Also remember that unless you're following Jesus, you'll be lost. His plan for your life is the only one that counts. The Bible is your road map for life, so make sure you know it well.

Always look for the best in people, and you'll end up discovering the best in yourself along the way. People may let you down and break your heart, but refuse to become bitter or cynical. You can rarely control what happens to you, but you can always control how you choose to respond. Always respond with grace, faith, dignity, patience, and perseverance.

Be the same person in both public and private. There's no true success without true integrity. Real success means living in a way that the people who know you the best are the ones who love and respect you the most.

Remember that every victory is an opportunity to give praise to God and to those who helped you achieve it, and every failure is an opportunity to gain new strength and perspective. Don't get too attached to your trophies, because you won't be able to take them with you. In the end, your relationships will be all that counts, so don't ever value finances over faith or possessions over people.

Don't build your identity on things that change (your looks, your money, your success), but build your identity on the only one who is unchanging. God's opinion of you is the only one that counts. He says you are limitlessly loved and called to a world-changing purpose, so don't settle for anything less.

Don't take yourself too seriously or your mission too lightly. Laughter and joy are gifts from God that should be cherished even in life's most challenging seasons. They're good medicine for the soul!

When you've blown it, be humble enough to admit fault and seek forgiveness. Pride has been the downfall of many men.

Be always confident, but never cocky. Be always aware, but never afraid. Be always content, but never complacent.

I love you guys more than you can imagine. Remember

that there's no mistake you could ever make that is bigger than God's grace. Your mom and I will always be your biggest fans!

Love,
Dad

DISCUSSION QUESTIONS

1. What life lessons (both positive and negative) did you learn in your family growing up?
2. What are the most important lessons you want to teach to your own children and grandchildren?
3. How would your family look different if every person always loved, trusted, and selflessly served the other family members?
4. What is one relationship within your family or extended family where you need to invest additional time and energy?

CHAPTER 10

LOVING YOUR NEIGHBOR

For the whole law can be summed up in this one
command: "Love your neighbor as yourself."

—GALATIANS 5:14

One of Jesus' most famous teachings centers around the concept of what it truly means to love your neighbor. When a teacher of the religious law asked Jesus to identify the most important commandment, Jesus, in his customary style, initially answered the question with another question. He asked the teacher to take a shot at answering.

The teacher said that the most important law was to love the Lord God with all your heart, mind, soul, and strength and then to love your neighbor as yourself. Jesus congratulated him on knowing the correct answer all along, but this teacher was apparently very concerned about his own image and ego, so he wanted to justify asking the question in the first place. He threw out a follow-up question: "Who is my neighbor?"

Jesus replied with a story about a traveler taking the dangerous road from Jerusalem to Jericho, where crime rates were high and the terrain was treacherous. This poor traveler fell into the hands of bandits, who robbed and beat him before leaving him for dead.

Now this poor man lay helpless and unconscious at the side of the road when a priest came upon him, but this pious passerby didn't want to get his hands dirty, so he just kept walking. A second religious leader also came by but was similarly too busy or too indifferent to stop and help.

Then a third person passed by, and he happened to be a Samaritan. Jesus was speaking to a Jewish audience who had deep-seated, generational prejudices against people from Samaria. Samaritans were considered the lowest rung on the societal ladder. Jews were raised to have nothing at all to do with them, and now Jesus was introducing a despised Samaritan as the hero.

The Samaritan in the story rushed to aid the injured Jewish man. He bandaged his wounds and carried him to his own donkey to transport him to an inn to recover. The Samaritan further promised the innkeeper he would return and assume all financial responsibility for the injured man's expenses.

As Jesus completed the scandalous story of the good Samaritan, he asked the teacher of the Jewish religious law which of the three passersby had been a neighbor to the injured man. The bewildered man had to give credit to the only one who stopped to help. Jesus agreed and told his listeners to go and be that kind of neighbor.

Over the past two thousand years, this simple story has been the inspiration for multiple charities, hospitals, and laws designed to heal and protect the wounded and powerless. Whether Jesus told this story as a real encounter or simply as a metaphor to illustrate a real truth is up for debate, but either way, the lesson is clear. We are called to love our neighbors, and one simple, selfless act of love has the power to change a life.

WHO ARE YOUR SAMARITANS?

Jesus made the Samaritan the hero of this story because he wanted to teach us that love is more powerful than prejudice. The first-century Jews who represented Jesus' community and family were elitist when it came to their race and religious heritage. Their national pride had slowly morphed into a distrust and disdain toward all other groups. In fact, some of the biggest struggles within the early church were the result of racial tensions and religious factions.

Two thousand years later, we haven't seemed to evolve all that much when it comes to our prejudices and racial divides. Had Jesus been telling the parable of the good Samaritan to today's audience, he may have made the story about "The Good Muslim" or "The Good Homosexual" or "The Good (fill in the blank with your own personal prejudice)."

This might be stepping on toes, but I'm talking to myself here as well. We all have our hidden prejudices about people we see as different from ourselves. We try to justify our lack of love toward them by arguing that they're sinners or wrong in their beliefs, and that may be true. But if love were only for perfect people, none of us would qualify. Loving someone doesn't mean you agree with everything that person does; it means your concern and commitment to that person is not conditional upon his or her behavior.

You may think you don't have any prejudices, but if you're human, you have prejudices. Perhaps you hold a profound prejudice toward those you perceive to be prejudiced in their views. That's pretty ironic, isn't it? You may not show outward signs of hostility toward certain people or groups of people, but your prejudices are displayed more by what you don't do. You don't pursue relationships with those people.

> LOVING SOMEONE DOESN'T MEAN YOU AGREE WITH EVERYTHING THAT PERSON DOES; IT MEANS YOUR CONCERN AND COMMITMENT TO THAT PERSON IS NOT CONDITIONAL UPON HIS OR HER BEHAVIOR.

If we want to identify our prejudices, all we need to do is ask ourselves which people or groups of people we avoid. Look at your list of friends on social media or the last party you hosted and ask yourself, *Which people or groups of people were absent? Who was uninvited?*

We can all be tempted to stay safely within the confines of our own communities and trust that someone else will reach those outsiders, but when we think this way, we're missing the point of what love is all about. Jesus came to break down the walls that people use to isolate themselves, and he intentionally built bridges where society had burned bridges. Some of Jesus' most famous conversations were with the outcasts of mainstream society.

Maybe you're reading this right now and you feel like an outsider. I think we've all felt that way at times, but some folks have had way more than their share of exclusion or even persecution. If that describes you, Jesus has a very special place in his heart for you. You are high on his guest list, and you are uniquely qualified to share his love with the world in profound ways.

We're all called to love neighbors who look nothing like we

look. Love can have its deepest impact in and through our lives

> LOVE CAN HAVE ITS DEEPEST IMPACT IN AND THROUGH OUR LIVES WHEN WE SHARE IT WITH THOSE OUTSIDE OF OUR OWN COMFORT ZONES.

when we share it with those outside of our own comfort zones. One of the most profound examples of this happened in my friend Larry's life. He courageously and selflessly loves his neighbors in ways that he never imagined would be possible until his life changed a few years ago.

NEIGHBORS BEHIND BARS

Larry is one of the toughest-looking guys I know. He looks like he's in a motorcycle gang and has the kind of beard that would make the guys on *Duck Dynasty* jealous. Larry has a tough exterior, but he's one of the most tenderhearted people on earth.

Several years ago, Larry was invited to become part of a prison ministry that went into local prisons to share the love and truth of Jesus with inmates. At first, Larry wasn't the least bit interested. He admitted that he had some prejudices toward prisoners because of the crimes they had committed to become incarcerated in the first place. On top of that, Larry had a full-time job and a family and was reluctant to give up so much time while putting himself in potentially dangerous situations.

As Larry was debating the choice, he was reminded about Jesus' teachings on what it means to be a good neighbor and how Jesus called us to be the light of the world, to reach out to the forgotten, including those in prison. One particular passage seemed to pierce Larry's heart when he read about Jesus saying that whatever we do for the hungry, oppressed, sick, impoverished, or imprisoned is an act we're actually doing for Jesus himself.

Larry decided that this was something he was going to do, but in his mind, it was going to be a one-time thing. Little did Larry know that God had much bigger plans. Larry's life was about to get very interesting.

In the years since Larry's first prison visit, he has now been to dozens of prisons, spoken to thousands of inmates, and seen hundreds of prisoners come to a life-changing faith in Jesus Christ. Larry doesn't take a penny for his ministry, but he drives great distances and invests hundreds of hours annually to serve imprisoned men who will never have a way to repay.

Larry just smiles and talks about what a blessing those prisoners have been to him. He has countless stories about lives that have been changed and moments that have changed his own life because of his decision to step out in faith and love his neighbors the way Jesus taught us to do.

One story that impacted him in a unique way is the story of a young man who was in prison for prostitution. We'll call him Tony. This young man had spent so much time on the streets dressed in drag that there were permanent marks from the makeup still visible on his face. Tony had lived his life far from God and didn't seem interested at all in the message of grace Larry was sharing.

Over time, a relationship developed, and the pain from Tony's past started unraveling as if the layers of an onion were being peeled away from his heart. Tony eventually came to a place of openness to the message Larry was sharing, and he surrendered his heart and life to Jesus.

Tony's transformation was radical. The guards and other

inmates noticed an immediate change. Tony's outlook on life became drastically different, and he started behaving like a man who had experienced true freedom for the first time in his life, even though he was still behind bars.

When the day of Tony's parole came, he left that prison a different man from the one who had entered several years earlier. Tony went back to his old neighborhood but refused to go back to living the same lifestyle. He was going to show his neighbors that a new life was possible for them as well because of the love and grace of Jesus.

Tragically, only three days after being released, Tony was stabbed to death in downtown Augusta, Georgia. The case remains a mystery, but it's believed that Tony may have been murdered by one of his former clients after refusing to engage in prostitution. It's quite possible that Tony died a martyr, trying to share the love of Jesus with someone who was violently opposed to the message.

Larry still cries when he talks about Tony, but through those tears he smiles, because he knows he'll see Tony again.

Larry also had the privilege of telling Tony's dad about his transformation. They had been estranged for a long time, but his dad cried tears of joy when Larry told him the story. He said, "I've been praying Tony would find Jesus for years. I'd given up hope, but God never gave up hope. This is a miracle."

Larry continues to travel to prisons several nights a week to build relationships with the men incarcerated there and share the message of true freedom that Tony and countless others have experienced through Christ. Larry is living out Jesus' command to love our neighbors as well as anyone I know, and his love for God and others continues to inspire and challenge all who know him.

WHEN YOU DON'T EVEN
KNOW YOUR NEIGHBOR

We're called to love our neighbors who live all over the world, but we can never overlook the neighbors who live right next door. I'm going to confess that this is very challenging for me. I'm writing a book on love and I preach to people on Sundays that they should love their neighbors, but I don't even know all of my neighbors.

Sometimes it feels easier for me to get on a plane to do a mission trip to a foreign land than it is to walk next door and have a meaningful conversation with my neighbor. I'm more introverted than people realize, and there are many days I just want to drive my car into the garage and wave at the strangers who live in the houses on my street without ever really engaging in meaningful conversations. I'm also reluctant to talk about what I do for a living, because as soon as people hear the words *pastor* or *church* they instantly start acting weird around me.

> WE'RE CALLED TO LOVE OUR NEIGHBORS WHO LIVE ALL OVER THE WORLD, BUT WE CAN NEVER OVERLOOK THE NEIGHBORS WHO LIVE RIGHT NEXT DOOR.

I want to throw out all these disclaimers like, "Well, I'm a pastor, but trust me, I'm actually a huge sinner," or "Well, technically I work at a church, but I'm remarkably normal."

I rarely give the disclaimers; I just embrace the weirdness. Truthfully, there's really not much of a stigma where I live. In my community, church is a normal part of life for many (if not most) families, and those who work in Christian ministry are respected much more here than they are in many places around the world. Still, I've never liked being seen as different, and there have been times when I've avoided pursuing deeper relationships with neighbors simply because I'm afraid of the weirdness that can sometimes happen.

This is an area where I've been challenged to get outside my comfort zone, because as I read the Bible and look at inspiring examples of people changing the world, I've noticed that nobody ever changed the world by staying safely in his or her comfort zone. God wants to stretch us. He wants us to trust him enough to get uncomfortable for the sake of sharing his love with a world that desperately needs it.

My wife and I decided that one practical way we could show love to our neighbors is to provide a safe and fun atmosphere where the neighbor kids can play. It also keeps our own kids close by, so we can keep a closer eye on them by being the house the kids want to visit instead of the house our own kids want to escape.

> GOD WANTS TO STRETCH US. HE WANTS US TO TRUST HIM ENOUGH TO GET UNCOMFORTABLE FOR THE SAKE OF SHARING HIS LOVE WITH A WORLD THAT DESPERATELY NEEDS IT.

We try to keep the doors open as often as possible while also making sure to have downtime, when we put a note on the front door saying the house is closed for the day. We throw a back-to-school bash every year when we spend our own money to get a bounce house, snow cone truck, and a bunch of food, and we invite anyone who will come just as a way to build relationships. It's amazing how much easier it is to build relationships with people when you're willing to feed and entertain them. I'll show up just about anywhere if there are free snacks involved.

Speaking of free snacks, we also try to keep the fridge stocked with fruit punch and snacks for the neighbor kids so that our own children can see firsthand how much we value serving others. Serving is often the first step in building meaningful relationships.

One day during snack time, I passed over the typical cheap stuff and pulled out some Lunchables. These weren't even the generic brand; they were the real deal with actual Oreo cookies for dessert and everything. This was a special snack. I don't know protocol for what food requires a prayer and what food doesn't, but it just seemed right to thank God for these Lunchables. I'm pretty sure God was behind the invention of Oreo cookies, and I wanted to pause and honor him before we devoured our treats.

Just before serving the Lunchables to our own boys and two other brothers from our neighborhood, I prayed for the snack and thanked God for the food and for each of our friends at the table by name. My prayer wasn't fancy or all that memorable. It went something like this: "God, you're awesome. We love you. We're really thankful for these delicious Lunchables and Oreo cookies we are about to eat. Thanks for such an awesome snack! Lord, I also want to thank you for our friends, Michael and Max. They're awesome boys. We're so glad that they're our friends. I ask that you'd bless these great boys and help them grow up to become men who will change the world for you. Thanks again for the Lunchables. In Jesus' name, amen."

Our two friends looked up from the prayer with a big smile on their faces, and the younger brother, Max, said, "Thanks!"

I said, "Oh, don't mention it. The Lunchables were on sale. They were only a buck apiece. No big deal."

He said, "No. I wasn't thanking you for the Lunchables. I mean, it's an awesome snack and I really appreciate it, but I was thanking you for the prayer." He looked at his brother, and then he looked back at me with an innocent radiance in his smile and said, "That's the first time anyone has ever said a prayer for us."

I smiled and told the boys that I'd be saying a lot of prayers for them and that we were so thankful that they were our friends.

I've reflected back on that moment often. God used that simple act as a reminder that we're in a world where people are hungry to experience the love of God, but often there's nobody in their lives willing to show it.

> WE CAN CHANGE THE WORLD WHEN WE'RE WILLING TO DO SMALL THINGS WITH LOVE.

That moment of enjoying a snack around our kitchen table and other moments like it have challenged me to keep my eyes open for small, everyday opportunities to show the big love of God. I often get so preoccupied with my own self-focused agenda, I miss out on the divine opportunities all around me. In our hurried world, it's easy to overlook the miracles hiding in plain sight. Still, we can change the world when we're willing to do small things with love.

WHEN NEIGHBORS ARE HARD TO LOVE

Ashley and I have had some wonderful neighbors through the years, but we've also had some neighbors we prayed would move to a different neighborhood. One of those extra-grace-required neighbors moved in next door one time with a pit bull who loved to bark all night long. I knew from the very first night that this was going to be a test of my faith.

I remember lying in my bed ready for a good night's sleep when the beast next door started barking like he was in a horror movie. Our windows were single-paned and our bedroom butted up to the neighbor's backyard, so I heard the dog as if he were standing right next to my bed all night. It was a frustrating evening to say the least.

Just as a quick public service announcement: if you have a dog you consistently keep outside even when the dog is barking, your neighbors might smile and wave at you when you drive by, but they all secretly wish you'd move away.

I tried to extend some grace that first night, because I figured the new neighbors were just getting settled in and they might have just forgotten to bring in the dog. Surely it wasn't going to be like this every night. I remember saying a prayer when my head hit the pillow the second night. I prayed for a peaceful and quiet night's sleep. It wasn't close to Christmastime, but I was humming "Silent Night" in my head and hoping for the best.

A few minutes of stillness in the bedroom were quickly shattered by the maniacal dog. I actually jumped out of bed and started throwing a temper tantrum. After a solid hour of listening to the barking, I finally decided to walk next door in my pajamas. I knocked on the door and politely asked my neighbor to put the dog indoors. She reluctantly agreed, and I went back to sleep.

The third night came around, and I assumed that after our understanding from the night before, this was no longer going to be an issue. I was wrong. The animal was on the loose again.

Night after night this pattern continued. Some nights I'd walk over and try to get her to put the dog indoors. Some nights I actually called the police and asked if they could come over and enforce the city noise ordinance. The whole situation was a nightmare. I get pretty grumpy when I can't get sleep.

Looking back on the whole ordeal, I believe God was using it to teach me patience and compassion. I never invested the time to get to know the woman next door the way I probably should have, but from my brief interactions with her, I knew she was a struggling single mom. She had come from a rough part of town, and the dog probably brought a sense of security for her and her small children.

I eventually determined that I was going to be the best neighbor I could be to that family. We encouraged our kids to play with her kids and tried to show kindness and thoughtfulness when we could. We helped clean up her yard when a tree fell, but, honestly, I had a hard time being neighborly. Just to confess, I actually failed many times when it came to being a good neighbor to her.

I prayed for my own sleep much more often than I prayed for her family. I worried about my own peace much more than I concerned myself with their security. I wanted them to move away much more than I wanted them to thrive.

We've since moved away from that neighborhood, but I still think back on the experience often. In fact, almost every time I hear a dog barking, I'm reminded that I'm called to love all my neighbors, not just the low-maintenance ones. I certainly don't claim to have it all figured out, but I'm convinced it doesn't have to be complicated. Loving our neighbors can start with small actions.

LOVING OUR NEIGHBORS CAN START WITH SMALL ACTIONS.

THERE'S ROOM FOR EVERYONE

My seven-year-old son, Connor, has such a big heart. He never wants anybody to be left out.

A few days ago we were watching one of his favorite cartoons,

Martha Speaks. It's about a dog named Martha who can talk. It's actually really entertaining. In this episode, Martha went to the dog pound to help with an adoption drive where they were trying to find a home for every dog in the pound. Martha was talking to all of the dogs, and each of them was so excited about the prospect of finding a new home. As the drive went on, most of the dogs were adopted, but one dog remained.

It was an old English bulldog named Pops. Not only was he rejected by all the families, but now he didn't even have his other friends with him in the pound anymore. When my son realized Pops was the only one left, tears started welling up in his eyes. I'm not going to lie . . . I was pretty sad too.

God never intended for any of us to walk alone. Our hearts should break for those who have been left out or rejected. God wants all of us in his family, where we are forever connected to him and to one another. He created the church to be a life-giving community and the hands and feet of Jesus to reach out to all who feel isolated or rejected. The bottom line is that God doesn't want anybody to feel like Pops! We all have a place in his family, and we should reach out to anyone who feels alone.

Maybe you feel like Pops. At one time or another, all of us have felt left out or rejected; but even in our loneliest moments, God is with us. Jesus promised to never leave us or forsake us. By the end of the episode, Pops was adopted. His story has a happy ending, and yours will, too, if you'll trust God and follow his timeless plan to live a life of love.

God's plan is for no one to walk alone. Just as he has reached out to us, we need to reach out to all those around us. We can't be selective or exclusive with our love for others, because every person on earth is our neighbor.

NEIGHBORS AROUND THE WORLD

I had the opportunity to travel to Haiti a few years ago just months after a devastating earthquake ravaged the impoverished island nation. The short time I spent there was life changing. I saw desperate poverty and powerful faith coexisting as thousands of Haitians with little food and no earthly possessions gripped tightly to the hope they had in Jesus that no earthquake could ever shake.

Each day my team would load up in the back of a truck and drive to our work sites, and every day along the way we would pass a small voodoo temple. Voodoo is still a dark and prevalent force in Haiti, and many have turned there for answers instead of turning to Christ. The voodoo priest there was a large, intimidating man who would stare us down each morning as we passed by. He seemed to be a man full of anger, and he apparently saw us (and our faith) as his enemy.

On our final day, we drove by and he wasn't there. Instead, there was a beautiful little girl who was maybe six years old standing where he would normally stand. She was dancing and smiling and waving to us. She seemed so innocent and full of life and possibility. I smiled and waved back at her, but as we drove away, the reality of what I had just seen began to set in.

I realized that little girl must have been the daughter of the angry voodoo priest who had made himself an enemy of God. In my mind, I started arguing with God, saying, "Lord, that little girl doesn't have any hope! She's beautiful and innocent, but she is surrounded by darkness. She has no future! She will never know you! Just look who her father is!"

I've never heard God audibly speak. I've always imagined he sounds like James Earl Jones, but I probably won't know for sure until I get to heaven. I didn't hear him speaking to me when we drove past that little girl, but I could sense in my spirit him gently whispering, "Her father is not a voodoo priest. Her father is the living God and Savior of the world. That little girl is *my* daughter, and the plans I have for her life are as beautiful as she is. There is no darkness that my light cannot penetrate. There is no evil that my goodness cannot replace. There is no person who is out of the reach of my loving hand."

I will probably never see that little girl again on this side of heaven, but I believe that God has extraordinary plans for her life. She is not just any anonymous face in a foreign land. She is our sister. She is our neighbor.

For her and for millions of children like her who are born in hostile situations, I pray that the love of God will break through and reach her. I pray that God's people will rise up and be the hands and feet of Jesus to extend God's grace and truth. I pray that we will be willing to go into the darkest places on earth to rescue people, because that is exactly what Jesus has already done for us.

> I PRAY THAT WE WILL BE WILLING TO GO INTO THE DARKEST PLACES ON EARTH TO RESCUE PEOPLE, BECAUSE THAT IS EXACTLY WHAT JESUS HAS ALREADY DONE FOR US.

DISCUSSION QUESTIONS

1. Who is the best neighbor you've ever had? Who is the worst neighbor?
2. What's the most thoughtful thing a neighbor has ever done for you?

3. How do you think we can best love our neighbors in our own neighborhoods?
4. How can we best love our neighbors on the other side of the world?
5. How would the world look different if we all truly loved our neighbors?

CHAPTER 11

LOVING YOUR FRIENDS

*A friend is always loyal, and a brother is born to help in
time of need.*

—PROVERBS 17:17

Some buddies of mine talked me into doing a Mud Run with
them. If you're unfamiliar with the concept, basically you
wake up early on a Saturday morning, put on some old clothes,
meet up with some friends, and spend several hours running
through mud, cold creeks, obstacles, and everything that nature
has to throw at you. It's crazy and painful and *awesome*! By the
end of it, you're exhausted, bloody, and muddy, but you feel an
unbelievable sense of accomplishment and shared victory with
the team who got you through it.

As I've been resting my aging body and reflecting back on
the experience, I've realized that this Mud Run has a lot of paral-
lels to life, faith, and friendship. There are going to be moments
when life is muddy, difficult, and filled with obstacles, but if we
don't quit, we can overcome together. Here are a few principles
that have come into focus for me:

1. We can't win alone.

Many of the obstacles on the course were designed to be impossible to accomplish without your team helping you out, and the race wasn't over until the entire team crossed the line. That's a beautiful picture of friendship. We don't win unless we win together, and we can't make it unless we're helping one another along the way. God never intended for any of us to run the race of life alone. He wants us to work together with him, and he is there by our side through it all, carrying us when necessary.

2. Shared struggles create strength.

Our tendency in life is to avoid obstacles and to complain when we have to face them, but in this race, the obstacles defined the experience. Never see your obstacles as punishments or curses but as opportunities to develop strength. Allow them to make you better, not bitter.

3. You can't lose if you don't quit.

The only way to fail the race is to quit, and in life and marriage, that same principle usually holds true. Don't give up! When you cross the finish line, you'll be so glad that you didn't give up. Quitting always leads to regret, but pushing through the pain and finishing strong always leads to joy.

4. The journey bonds you together.

My buddies and I are closer than ever because we conquered the course together. If we would have just spent the morning sipping coffee and talking about sports, the day would have already been forgotten, but now we have an epic experience to share for years to come.

Whatever challenges you are facing right now in your relationships, finances, health, or life in general, tackle those trials with courage, and be willing to get muddy and bloody along the way. Our greatest breakthroughs usually happen outside our comfort zones. Once you cross the finish line, I can guarantee that you will feel incredible!

WE ALL NEED A FRIEND

Jimmy's dad was in the military, so like most military families, Jimmy's family had to move often. He had already been to several elementary schools, and now he was preparing to be the new kid again.

Jimmy was in the garage looking at his cherished comic book collection and trying to make conversation with his dad while his father went through the familiar routine of unpacking boxes in a new house.

"Hey, Dad, do you want to look at my comic books with me?"

Jimmy's dad was tired from the move and focused on the task at hand. We dads can get pretty task-driven sometimes. He smiled and said, "Buddy, I'm really busy right now. Can you let me finish unpacking these boxes?"

Jimmy respectfully replied, "Yes, sir. Of course."

Jimmy watched his dad continue the unpacking a minute longer, and then he spoke again. "Dad, could I stay here and talk with you while you're unpacking the boxes?"

"Sure, Jimmy. That would be fine."

Jimmy smiled and pulled out his comic books. Thumbing through the pages, Jimmy asked a profound question: "Dad, who would you rather be: Batman or Superman?"

Grown men still ponder questions like these, so Jimmy's dad stopped his chores to think before responding. He finally answered, "Hmm, I think I'd be Superman. I've always liked Superman."

"Awesome, Dad! I've always liked Superman too. Why would you be Superman?"

"I'd be Superman because he can fly. I think it'd be pretty cool to fly."

"Totally! It would be awesome to fly."

"What about you, Jimmy? Who would you be?"

Jimmy looked down at his comic books and saw Superman flying through the air and Batman and Robin running into battle together. "I'd definitely be Batman."

"That's great, Jimmy. Why would you want to be Batman?"

> FLYING ALONE IS NOTHING COMPARED TO WALKING ALONGSIDE A REAL FRIEND.

Jimmy's answer almost brought tears to his dad's eyes. He held up the picture of Batman and Robin, and with awe and innocence in his voice, Jimmy said, "I'd be Batman because Batman has a friend."

We all need a friend. Jimmy wanted a friend more than he wanted to be able to fly. Flying alone is nothing compared to walking alongside a real friend.

HOW TO BE A FRIEND

The book of Proverbs teaches that the key to having friends is to simply be friendly. That's a profoundly simple thought, and yet, we seem to have lost sight of it through the years.

Being nice to people isn't a personality trait; it's a choice. We don't always feel like being nice, but it's always worth the effort. It communicates our respect for the people around us, and it ultimately brings joy to ourselves, encouragement to others, and glory to our creator.

Sadly, our culture seems to be moving away from valuing friendliness. We actually avoid one another. Instead of big front porches, we build houses with big back porches and tall privacy fences. Privacy has its place, but we need to be intentional about building relationships with people.

One thing I have learned in life and ministry is that it's not about the tasks; it's about the people. The better we are at interacting with people, the better we'll be at our work and most every other part of our lives. I definitely don't claim to have all the answers when it comes to people skills, but here are a few simple principles I've learned along the way that help as we seek to make new friends:

1. Smile.

When you smile, it makes you more pleasant to look at (even if your teeth are messed up like many of my relatives in Kentucky). It's disarming and usually makes the people around you feel more comfortable.

2. Make eye contact.

When you're looking at someone and not constantly looking around or looking at your watch, it communicates to the person in front of you that you genuinely value and respect him or her. Even if you're in a hurry, don't act like it. Make that person believe that there's no place on earth more important in that moment than being there with him or her. Being fully present requires eye contact.

3. Be enthusiastic and warm even when you don't feel like it.

Every time you see someone, convince that person and convince yourself that you're genuinely happy to see him or her. When we run into someone and we're not in the mood to talk, it's usually written all over our faces and conveyed through our body language, and it creates a tense and awkward conversation that both parties want to escape. When you rise above how you're feeling and respond to the person with warmth and enthusiasm, your feelings will usually catch up to your actions, and you'll end up having an encouraging conversation that you both will enjoy.

4. Be courteous with technology.

This is a *huge* one. In our age of smartphones, there's a whole new set of rules for what's acceptable and polite in conversation. Just a few general rules: Don't check your phone in the middle of a conversation unless you are expecting an important call. Talking with the person in front of you is always more important than texting with somebody else. Also, if someone calls you, don't return that person's call with a text or an e-mail. I know it's tempting and it's a time-saver, but if he or she called you, have the courtesy to call that person back.

5. Actually listen to what the other person is saying.

Instead of just nodding and smiling and planning an exit strategy, make a genuine effort to listen and respond with thoughtfulness. Repeat parts of what the other person has said, and ask specific questions as a follow-up to your last conversation with him or her to let that person know that you remember and care about what's important to him or her.

6. Use first names.

When you take the time to learn someone's name, it shows that you care. We've all been guilty of saying, "Hey, bro!" or "What's up, girl!" as a substitute, but whenever possible, learn to use the other person's name. It will make a big difference.

CHOOSE WISELY

The Bible teaches us that bad company corrupts good character (1 Cor. 15:33). God calls us to love everyone and be friendly to all people, but you must also have the wisdom to choose wisely when it comes to choosing your close friends. They will have a tremendous influence in your life. We become like our friends. It's as simple as that.

This is a lesson we as parents teach our kids, but we often don't apply these principles to our own lives. Invest in relationships where you're improved in the process. If someone is consistently a negative influence, it might be time for you to put some space between yourself and that person.

This isn't about being elitist or judgmental. This is being practical. You only have so many minutes in a day, and every minute you spend with a person is a minute you're choosing not to spend with every other person in your life. Are you following me? Don't spend your precious time and energy investing in negative relationships when you have real friends and family members who would love to be spending that time with you.

> IF SOMEONE IS CONSISTENTLY A NEGATIVE INFLUENCE, IT MIGHT BE TIME FOR YOU TO PUT SOME SPACE BETWEEN YOURSELF AND THAT PERSON.

A real friend is someone who will make you better. I've been blessed to have some wonderful friends through the years. I think about my college friend Charlie who would force me to get out of bed in the morning to go the gym with him. If I wouldn't wake up, he'd put on one of the *Rocky* movies to get me motivated. If that didn't work, he'd jab me with insults until I finally got up.

I would have been much fatter in college if it wasn't for Charlie, but he didn't just push me physically. He also challenged me spiritually. His faith in God and love for people challenged me to be more compassionate. I became a better person because he was my friend. That's the kind of friend I hope to be. We all need friends like that.

> SURROUND YOURSELF WITH PEOPLE WHO STRENGTHEN YOUR CHARACTER, AND REMOVE YOURSELF FROM PEOPLE WHO COMPROMISE YOUR CHARACTER.

Be that kind of friend, and choose those kinds of friends. Sharpen one another. Encourage one another. Surround yourself with people who strengthen your character, and remove yourself from people who compromise your character.

THE LITMUS TEST OF FRIENDSHIP

What does it mean to be a real friend? How can you tell who your real friends are? Is every Facebook friend a true friend?

Healthy friendships are vital to life, so it's important that we have good friends and that we become good friends to others. Here are a few key traits that should be present in any healthy friendship. These are straight from the Bible, so you can use these as a checklist in your own friendships to make sure you and your friends are on a healthy track.

1. Friends forgive.

Friends don't bring up old dirt and gossip about each other. They forgive and seek forgiveness with transparency and humility.

"Love prospers when a fault is forgiven, but dwelling on it separates close friends" (Prov. 17:9).

2. Friends love unconditionally.

They are there for you when you need them most, not just when it's convenient. We should love each other with the same kind of love God has shown to us.

"Dear friends, since God loved us that much, we surely ought to love each other" (1 John 4:11).

3. Friends have your back.

Loyalty is vital to friendship. There's no such thing as a "frenemy."

"There are 'friends' who destroy each other, but a real friend sticks closer than a brother" (Prov. 18:24).

4. Friends tell you the truth.

Even when it's hard to hear, friends will speak the truth in love. An enemy will tell you what you want to hear but won't love you enough to tell you a difficult truth.

"An honest answer is like a kiss of friendship" (Prov. 24:26).

5. Friends make each other better.

Friends don't pull each other down; they lift each other up. They encourage one another toward continuous improvement.

"As iron sharpens iron, so a friend sharpens a friend" (Prov. 27:17).

6. Friends communicate openly.

Friends communicate openly, honestly, and respectfully.

"I no longer call you slaves, because a master doesn't confide in his slaves. Now you are my friends, since I have told you everything the Father told me" (John 15:15).

UNLIKELY BUDDIES

Much of what the Bible teaches us about friendship is recorded in the book of Proverbs, which was written by King Solomon. Solomon was King David's son, and I'm sure Solomon learned a lot of his friendship wisdom from his dad.

King David had one of the most famous and most unlikely friendships in the Bible. Before he was king, he befriended another young warrior named Jonathan. Jonathan's dad was King Saul, the king before David.

I want you to grasp the tension here. David was anointed to be the next king of Israel instead of Jonathan, who was the presumed heir to the throne as King Saul's firstborn son. David and Jonathan had so many reasons to be jealous and distrusting of each other. They could have allowed pride and vanity to get in the way, but they didn't.

On multiple occasions, they each put their own lives on the line to protect each other. They forged a powerful bond of trust and brotherhood. They may have been the original BFFs.

Their friendship was so pure and so special because they remained focused on God over selfish pride and on their friendship over personal gain. Instead of looking for ways to surpass each other, they were always looking for ways to be a blessing to each other. This is a hallmark of pure friendship.

LOVE AND AVAILABILITY

When we love people, we make it a priority to be present with them. True friendship requires availability. We aren't just there in the moments that are convenient for us; we're also there in moments that are important for them. My mom is a great example of this principle.

Mom understands that time is the currency of relationships, and an investment in a relationship requires an investment in time. She has carried this principle into all of her friendships, which is why she has maintained a healthy and vibrant group of lifelong friends (which is exceptionally rare and hard to do).

TIME IS THE CURRENCY OF RELATIONSHIPS.

As we were growing up, she always gave us uninterrupted time and made us feel significant and secure because of her attentiveness. A generation later, she continues to selflessly invest in her grandchildren, her family, and her friendships. Dad did the same by taking time off work to coach us in sports and sacrificing to invest in his family and friendships. She and Dad not only taught us to love Jesus, but they showed us what it means to love *like* Jesus.

Jesus perfectly modeled genuine love through availability everywhere he went. One of the ways he consistently conveyed love was through simply being present with people. His availability showed his heart. Sure, Jesus would take time alone to pray, but he never stayed in solitude very long. He was always ready for the next opportunity to engage with people.

Reading about Jesus' consistent availability for people challenges me, because some days I have to fight the temptation to hide behind a computer screen instead of searching for meaningful interactions. When I do interact, my selfish nature often pulls me toward people who would be good networking contacts. In other words, I'm drawn to people who could help me in some way.

There's nothing wrong with networking, but there is a huge difference between networking and love. Networking is about doing for others so that you'll be repaid in some way; love is about serving others even when they're in no position to repay you. Jesus was completely available and attentive to people who had no way to repay him. That's the essence of love.

> JESUS REALIZED THAT PEOPLE AREN'T INTERRUPTIONS TO OUR AGENDAS; PEOPLE *ARE* THE AGENDA!

Jesus realized that people aren't interruptions to our agendas; people *are* the agenda! He made himself available to meet people right where they were.

A guy in the Bible who learned this lesson in dramatic fashion was a social outcast named Zacchaeus. He was a tax collector in Israel during a time when the label of "tax collector" brought some deep-seated social stigmas. His profession made him despised among his people. His fellow Israelites looked at him like a traitor because he was profiting from the extortion of his own people in order to funnel tax revenue to the occupying Roman government.

As you can imagine, Zacchaeus didn't have many friends. He was rich, but he was incredibly lonely. There wasn't much direction or purpose to his life. He had discovered that if life's only about money, there's not enough money in the world to fill the God-sized void in the human soul. He thought wealth would bring him happiness, but he learned the painful truth epitomized in the rap lyrics of the Notorious B.I.G. when he said, "Mo money, mo problems."

Zacchaeus didn't know where to turn for hope. I'm sure he wondered if his life would ever have significance. He might have been riding on the nicest donkey in town, but he was riding on a very lonely road.

All that changed the day Zacchaeus met Jesus.

Jesus was passing through town, and Zacchaeus was desperate to meet him. The rich tax collector pursued Jesus with the tenacity of a preteen girl seeking an autograph at a One Direction concert. Zacchaeus's life had been building up to this moment, but because he was such a short man, he couldn't see over the crowd to get to Jesus. Undaunted by the challenges and unafraid to look ridiculous, Zacchaeus scurried up a sycamore fig tree to get a better view.

Jesus stopped and looked up at the tiny man hanging from the branch. He knew Zacchaeus was there. Jesus called him down from the tree and the two men went to Zacchaeus's house to share a meal together.

That encounter with Jesus changed Zacchaeus's life. This despised tax collector became passionately committed to restoring broken relationships. Jesus helped him see clearly that money alone never makes for a successful life. A successful life requires love: love for God, love for yourself, and love for others.

Clarence, in the classic film *It's a Wonderful Life*, said, "No man is poor who has friends."

Zacchaeus learned the same lesson the day he became friends with Jesus. He was rich financially but poor relationally. Discovering the grace, love, and friendship Jesus offered unlocked the key to true riches. You can't put a price tag on friendship.

LOOK FOR WAYS TO BE A BLESSING

Last night I took my kids to McDonald's for a Happy Meal. We were on our way to a flag football game and were in a hurry, so I didn't inspect the contents of our order until we were back on the road and I heard my boys giggling as they pulled out their Happy Meal toys. "It's Hello Kitty! It's a girl toy!"

The folks at the drive-through window had given us girl toys by mistake. The boys laughed and joked for a moment, expecting me to pull out the real toys, but when I told them those were the only toys, their moods became more serious. They were angry! They acted like their meals had been laced with leprosy and that girl cooties might have somehow infected their french fries. They tossed the helpless Hello Kitty toys on the floorboard of the van in rebellion and disgust.

GIVING TO A FRIEND IS ALWAYS MORE REWARDING THAN HOARDING FOR OURSELVES.

I tried to think of a life lesson to share with them. Honestly, I wasn't doing it to be a good father or because I'm a preacher and that's what preachers are supposed to do. I was just frustrated, running late, and tired of hearing them complain, but in the end, I think God taught us all an important lesson. I asked the boys if they knew any little girls at school who might like the toys. Maybe God gave them the girl toys because they weren't meant for them but to be given to a friend.

They immediately started talking about the girls in their class who would love the Hello Kitty toys. As I helped them plan, they started enjoying the anticipation of giving the toys away even more than they would have enjoyed the action figures they were supposed to get. Giving to a friend is always more rewarding than hoarding for ourselves.

I believe that very often God puts gifts in our lives that aren't there for our own personal consumption; but because we're all pretty selfish by nature, we disregard those gifts as trash instead of thinking about how we could bless someone else with them. We miss the opportunity to encourage. We also rob ourselves of the blessing that always comes when we selflessly give to a friend.

What in your life do you have but don't really need? There's someone out there who would be blessed to receive it. Don't hoard it; don't throw it away. Choose to give it. Not only will you bless someone else, you'll be blessed too. Always look for practical ways to enrich the lives of your friends.

DISCUSSION QUESTIONS

1. Who was your best friend when you were growing up?
2. Who would you consider your best friend today? What qualities make that person such a good friend?
3. What do you believe are the factors that separate friends from acquaintances?
4. What's one way you could do a better job loving your friends?

CHAPTER 12

LOVING YOUR ENEMIES

You have heard the law that says, "Love your neighbor"
and hate your enemy. But I say, love your enemies! Pray
for those who persecute you!

—MATTHEW 5:43–44

I love the Bible, but I don't understand all of it. There are some parts in Scripture where I'll read it and reread and I'm still scratching my head, having absolutely no idea what it means. As a pastor, this makes me a little insecure when someone comes up to me with questions about an obscure passage from Revelation or wants to talk to me about Blood-Moon Prophecies.

In those situations, I usually just nod my head and hope they don't figure out that I have no idea what they're talking about. Ironically, it's not the parts of the Bible I don't understand that bother me most. The parts of the Bible that really bother me are the words I do understand and simply don't like.

When Jesus gave us the command to "love your enemies" (Matt. 5:44), there was no mistaking what he was talking about.

He was clear and consistent in his message and in his actions. He didn't just teach us to love our enemies, but he modeled what it looks like to do it. While Jesus was being nailed to a cross, tortured to death by callous Roman soldiers and mocked by the so-called religious elite who had put the whole execution in motion, Jesus prayed for the very people who were killing him.

That kind of love is usually where we draw the line. We're all for loving our friends and our relatives and even extending grace when they make a mistake, but we won't even entertain the idea of giving love to people who would hate or harm us. Surely, Jesus didn't really mean for us to do that, did he? I mean, we can't go around trying to give hugs and kisses to murderers, right?

At most, we'll show tolerance to our enemies. *Tolerance* has become a political buzzword that supposedly means that we should be so open-minded that we'll put up with anybody, but tolerance has nothing to do with love. Jesus raised the bar because he never taught us to tolerate people; he taught us to love people. Tolerance simply masks our prejudices, but love destroys our prejudices.

The truth is that Jesus wants us to love our enemies, and it's not just for the sake of our enemies. God loves you too much to let you go through life with a heart full of bitterness. Bitterness and love can't live in the same heart. Each day you've got to decide which one gets to stay.

DON'T TREAT PEOPLE THE WAY THEY TREAT YOU; TREAT PEOPLE THE WAY GOD TREATS YOU.

When you love those who are hostile in return, you're doing it as an offering to God. Don't treat people the way they treat you; treat people the way God treats you. Show respect even to those who don't deserve it, not as a reflection of their character, but as a reflection of yours.

CHOOSING BETWEEN LOVE AND BITTERNESS

Derek Elam and I grew up together. He was a couple years younger than me, but he was the kind of kid who could instantly befriend kids and adults of all ages. It was rare for him to meet someone he didn't like or someone who didn't like him. He seemed to have no enemies.

In 2004, Derek was young, strong, smart, talented, ambitious, and ready to take on the world. He was preparing to move from our hometown of Georgetown, Kentucky, to Nashville, Tennessee. Nashville might not seem like a huge city for you, but for country kids like us, moving to Nashville was the equivalent of moving to New York City or Los Angeles. We were all excited for him and a little jealous at the same time.

Friday, July 2, was only a few weeks away from his twenty-third birthday and his planned move. Derek had scheduled to be off work so he could hang out with family and friends, but he decided at the last minute to pick up a few more shifts at the music store where he had worked near the University of Kentucky's campus to make some last-minute cash to take to Tennessee.

He was manning the cash register on a quiet Tuesday afternoon, selling records and CDs (which, for you younger readers, is what we used to have in the old days before iTunes was invented). I'm sure he was enjoying the day the way he seemed to always enjoy life. He had no way of knowing that he was about to come face-to-face with the most dangerous enemy he would ever encounter.

A man burst through the door and put a gun in Derek's face. He demanded all the money in the cash register. Derek immediately emptied the cash register and held his hands in the air, but the thief still put the .22-caliber gun to Derek's head and pulled the trigger. With my friend lying on the floor in a pool of his own blood, the gunman fled with the cash. It was less than one hundred dollars.

I received the shocking phone call from my old buddy, Adam, who had been in the church youth group with Derek and me. I rushed to the hospital as fast as I could drive and walked into that emotionally charged ICU waiting room to see Derek's family and many friends crying, hoping and praying for a miracle.

I made my way through the maze of chaos and found the room where he was on life-support. I'll never forget that crushing feeling of seeing a friend who had been so full of life now lying lifeless in a hospital bed. It didn't seem real. It didn't seem possible. And yet, it had happened, and there was no way to undo it. Derek died that night.

This story would be unimaginably tragic if this were the end of the story, but because of what Jesus has done on our behalf, death is never the end of the story.

Derek's mom, Diana, had always had a strong faith, but we never really know how strong our faith is until it's tested by tragedy. Here in the midst of the worst tragedy a parent could ever experience, she exuded a peace that couldn't be explained apart from God. Through her tears, she comforted others. She smiled as she talked about how Derek was now with Jesus. She reassured us all that death wasn't the end of this story and we would see him again.

She carried that same attitude into the funeral. She chose

to wear white. She said that while it was a heartbreaking day for us, it was a glorious day for Derek, because he was now home in heaven where there's no more pain or sickness or crime or death. With a broken heart, she found the strength to give thanks to God in her darkest hour.

The grieving process for most of us was a combination of sadness and anger. We felt sadness over the unspeakable loss and anger due to the senseless act of violence that caused it. We all wanted justice, and we wanted it fast. The city rallied together, and a manhunt ensued for Derek's killer.

It wasn't long before the perpetrator was apprehended. He was a young man about Derek's age. He had recently been released on parole for another murder he had committed as a juvenile, and now he was a repeat offender who had committed murder on two separate occasions. If there was ever a person who deserved to be hated, it had to be him.

As much temptation and justification as there might have been for hatred, Derek's mom chose a different path. She wisely realized that bitterness doesn't exist in a vacuum. When we harbor a grudge toward someone, it doesn't stay isolated to the person who wronged us. It always spills over and eventually harms our friends and family as well.

> BITTERNESS SPREADS RAPIDLY, BUT THANKFULLY, SO DOES LOVE.

Bitterness spreads rapidly, but thankfully, so does love. Diana refused to have a bitter heart. Of course, she wanted justice for her son, but hatred has nothing to do with justice. She refused to hate the man who murdered Derek. She chose instead to respond with love.

She prayed for this man. She prayed for his conviction, but she also prayed for his salvation. She prayed that God would give her the strength to not only forgive him but to love him. In a supernatural way, God granted her prayer and changed her heart. She no longer saw the man as a monster. She saw him as a lost and wounded child who desperately needed the love and grace of his heavenly Father.

Ultimately, the courts did their job, and justice was carried out. He was convicted and sentenced to life in prison, but Diana's faith and love continues to extend to the man who killed her son. Her faith has inspired many. Below is her summation of all that's happened in her own words.

I continue to pray he (Derek's murderer) will come to know Jesus and ask God to let me know when that happens. I had a dream one night shortly after this happened that he and Derek were in heaven together and he apologized to Derek. Derek said, "You're here in heaven. That's what matters." I knew that was God's way of saying this will come to pass. I forgave him the minute I knew of this murder but also believe he should serve out his life in prison. Without Christ, he's a dead man walking no matter where he is. With Christ, he's free no matter where he is. Because I gave this over to God and let him handle it all, I was free of bitterness, anger, unforgiveness, and grudges, which are the fruit of our enemy. Instead God gave me the ability to walk in his fruit of love, joy, peace, patience, kindness, gentleness, faithfulness, and self-control. I am free indeed thanks to our wonderful heavenly Father.

Most of us will probably never encounter the kind of enemy who will threaten our lives or the lives of our children, but there will still be people who hurt you. When you experience the sting of betrayal or rejection, human nature will tempt you to retaliate with revenge, but God has a different and better path for you. When we choose to trust him with the justice part, we can focus on the business of healing and promoting love.

In his journal, shortly before he died, Derek wrote that he wanted his life to be a "light shining for all eternity."

Diana had that phrase carved into his tombstone. This family's legacy of love and faith is indeed a light that has pierced even the darkest places of our world. Their legacy is a testament to the seventh Law of Love: love lives forever.

LOVING THE UNLOVABLE

Even if we are never put in a position where we have to face our child's murderer, as Derek's parents did, we'll all eventually be put in positions where we are called to love those who aren't being lovable. They'd be easier to avoid than to love, but I believe God has a very special place in his heart for unlovable people, and we should too. It helps when we remember that we're all unlovable at times.

> GOD HAS A VERY SPECIAL PLACE IN HIS HEART FOR UNLOVABLE PEOPLE, AND WE SHOULD TOO.

One of my favorite stories in the Bible takes place in John chapter 8. A woman who had been caught in the act of adultery was dragged out into the streets for the public execution of her reputation and her body. In this culture, it was legal to kill a woman who committed adultery, and the self-righteous mob was about to carry out the sentence.

As they threw her onto the ground in front of Jesus, the

people realized they could now kill two birds with one stone. They could quench their bloodlust and also discredit Jesus by trapping him in an unwinnable argument. Little did they know that they were picking a fight with the wrong guy.

They gave Jesus a quick lesson on Old Testament law and explained how this woman had sinned and was worthy of death. But Jesus seemed unimpressed by their righteous indignation. Maybe it was because of the sexist nature of the law's enforcement. Why was it only the woman was here? Doesn't it take two people to commit adultery?

Perhaps Jesus looked through their charade and saw their hypocrisy. He saw the mountain of sin in each of their lives. Maybe he looked straight at this woman and saw the brokenness of her past. He didn't just see her sin; he saw her.

He stood up from where he had been writing in the sand and proclaimed this judgment on the situation: "Whoever is without sin can throw the first stone at her."

One by one, the others dropped their stones and walked away until only Jesus and the woman remained. He was the only one there without sin, and he never picked up a rock. Instead, he told her to go and sin no more. Jesus offers us the same grace, and he commands us to offer that same grace and love to others.

As Mother Teresa once said, "If you judge people, you have no time to love them."

THERE'S ALWAYS MORE TO THE STORY

My Aunt Laurie is one of the most lovable people you'll ever meet. She has a contagious joy, and her laughter fills the room from the moment she walks in the door. Even now, as I'm writing these words and thinking about her, I'm smiling. To know her is to love her, but she wasn't always so lovable. In fact, there was a very dark time in her life when she was unrecognizable from the warm and joyful person she is today.

Decades ago, she was addicted to cocaine and meth, was a convicted felon, and was involved in a string of dysfunctional relationships with some dangerous men. If you had met her back in that season of her life, you probably would have passed by on the other side of the street. You wouldn't have wanted to get too close. You may have shaken your head in disapproval and labeled her as a "junkie" or a "criminal," and on the surface, your judgment would have been correct. But there's always more to the story than what we can see on the surface.

Aunt Laurie wasn't always a junkie. In fact, the dark circumstances that led her down that destructive road can be traced back to a single moment on a day that tragically changed her life forever. I was only five years old, but I remember the moment vividly. I remember it, because it was the first time I ever saw my father cry.

Aunt Laurie and her family were enjoying a beautiful summer day out on the river. Her daughter, Teana, climbed up on the bow to look up at her dad, but she slipped and fell in. Her dad, my Uncle Dean, heard the splash and instinctively did what any father would do; he jumped in after his little girl. The river's current was too strong. They both drowned that day.

A few days later we faced the kind of funeral you pray your family never has to experience. Dean and Teana were placed in the same coffin, and when my aunt saw the body of her husband holding the body of her little girl, something inside her broke. It was the kind of pain no human heart could possibly endure. When she made the decision to turn to drugs for the first time, it wasn't so she could feel high; it was so she could feel numb.

Now, does her tragedy justify her sin? No. But knowing her story changes something. Doesn't it?

It reminds us that hurting people in this world need our love, not our judgment. They need our support, not our condemnation.

So, how does this apply to your life and relationships?

Here are a few principles to keep in mind when it comes to loving the unlovable. If you'll apply these to your relationships, I believe you can be part of changing someone's life in the moments when he or she may need it most:

1. Don't treat people the way they treat you; treat people the way God treats you.

The character of God is to give love to unlovable people, and *all* of us have been unlovable people. His love makes all love possible. The more you love God and embrace his love and grace in your life, the more capacity you will have to give love and grace to others.

2. Invest in people at strategic low points.

Every financial advisor will tell you that if you want to maximize your investment on a stock, you need to invest when the stock is low, not when it's high. Sure, there's risk in investing at low points, but risk is just a part of life. When it comes to relational investing, I believe this same principle holds true. If you want to maximize your positive impact in someone's life, don't invest in the relationship only when the other person is on top of the world (high points). Give that person your best when his or her stock is low. Serve her when she has no way to repay you. Be willing to rush into his pain and tragedy when everyone else is rushing out. You'll be part of changing that person's life while also building a lifelong bond in the relationship. That's real love.

3. Expect nothing in return.

This part is really hard, because we want everything we give to eventually be reciprocated. But that's not always how love works. If we show kindness only to get kindness in return, we're not showing love; we're networking to get ahead. Give your best even when it's not reciprocated. Jesus did that for us, and he calls us to do it for each other.

4. Balance tough love with compassion.

When the people we love are in a self-destructive cycle and they're a potential harm to themselves or to others, there may be times to show tough love. Depending on the circumstances, this may require interventions or even legal action, but make sure your motives are always driven by a deep and abiding compassion for the well-being of everyone involved.

5. Don't quit on them, and don't let them quit on themselves.

The Bible teaches that there is nothing we could ever do that could possibly separate us from God's love (Rom. 8:38–39). God calls us to have that same limitless love for others. It's a love that's not based on our own strength; it's made possible only because of his strength. Once someone realizes that you're going to stick with him or her no matter what, it can give that person the strength to persevere.

DISCUSSION QUESTIONS

1. Who has been the most difficult person in your life to love?
2. How do you define an "enemy"? Why do you think Jesus taught so specifically that we should show love (not just tolerance) to enemies?
3. During what time in your life were you most unlovable? Who still showed you love during that time?
4. Did your perspective about Aunt Laurie change after hearing her story? Why do you think knowing someone's story changes how we see that person?

CHAPTER 13

LOVING YOURSELF

You made all the delicate, inner parts of my body and
knit me together in my mother's womb. Thank you for
making me so wonderfully complex! Your workmanship is
marvelous—how well I know it.

—PSALM 139:13–14

I vividly remember my first big prayer as a kid. I had just watched the original Superman movie with Christopher Reeve and immediately knew my destiny. I was going to be a superhero! All I needed was some tights, a cool name, some hair gel, and, of course, the ability to fly. I was pretty sure I could get most of the stuff on my own, but flight was going to be a problem.

I had just learned in Sunday school that if you pray in Jesus' name, God would give you whatever you asked for. That sounded like my ticket to flight! I stood up on a big rock in our backyard, and I looked around to make sure none of the neighbors were looking. Then I closed my eyes as tightly as I could and mustered up the best prayer a five-year-old could make.

"God, please let me fly like Superman! In Jesus' name I pray, amen!"

I felt a surge of adrenaline pump through my tiny body, and I raised my arms to the heavens and leaped off that rock. You will never guess what happened next. I flew!

Okay, I didn't actually fly. In reality, I fell to the ground and scraped up my knees and my childlike faith.

I was so confused. I thought prayer was supposed to work! I thought that God wanted to give us the desires of our hearts, and I had never wanted anything as badly as I wanted to be a superhero. I thought maybe I had prayed wrong, or maybe God was mad at me for something. Maybe I was never meant to be a superhero, and I just needed to lower my standards and give up on my dreams.

That disappointing moment stuck with me, and I came to a place where I subconsciously lowered my standards and decided not to expect too much out of life. Sadly, I think that's where most people get stuck. We start out in life with all kinds of hopes and dreams and unbridled energy, but along the way the disappointments replace our dreams with disillusionment. It was never meant to be this way.

All of those hopes and dreams that God placed inside you as a kid are desires he still wants to fulfill. Your destiny won't look exactly like you imagined (there probably won't be tights involved), but your reality can be something even better than you imagined.

GOD CREATED YOU TO BE A SUPERHERO! HE MADE YOU TO CHANGE THE WORLD.

Here's the bottom line: God created you to be a superhero! He made you to change the world. You were never meant to be a spectator in life, just going through the motions and barely getting by; you are meant to be a courageous agent of change, fulfilling a God-given destiny that will impact eternity.

God's perfect plan for transforming our lives doesn't require tights or a cape or the ability to fly. It requires love. You were born to live a life of love! Love God, love others, and yes, love yourself.

KAIZEN

I learned a powerful lesson about life and love in a very unlikely place. When I was in college, I worked the night shift for two summers at a Toyota plant in Georgetown, Kentucky. I didn't enjoy the vampire schedule of sleeping during the day and staying up all night, but I was making more than double the minimum wage, so for a college kid, I felt like I'd hit the jackpot. While my friends were eating ramen noodles, I was feasting like a king on pizza and Taco Bell. Life was good.

As valuable as that paycheck was to me, the most valuable asset I took away from that experience wasn't the money but a single word and the philosophy around it. It's a word that would have a transformative impact on my future marriage, career, and every other important aspect of my life. It was the Japanese word *kaizen*, which has guided Toyota and countless companies around the world. The word simply means "to improve continuously."

I was pulled into a culture where, even though profits were already high and the operation was already running smoothly, nobody was content to rest on past successes. There was a constant and continuous movement toward improvement, which impacted every aspect of the company and every individual within it. Finding ways to shave even a fraction of a second off the assembly process could mean the difference of millions of dollars over the period of a few years. Every improvement, big or small, was implemented and celebrated.

Kaizen shouldn't be used just to build better cars; it should be leveraged to build better relationships. Even the tiniest of positive changes, implemented consistently over time, has the power to produce a completely new reality. I want you to imagine how your life would look if each day you found a way to make your relationships a little better than they were the day before. Imagine how every aspect of your life could improve in the process. It's possible, and it's completely within your power to make it a reality.

> EVEN THE TINIEST OF POSITIVE CHANGES, IMPLEMENTED CONSISTENTLY OVER TIME, HAS THE POWER TO PRODUCE A COMPLETELY NEW REALITY.

Continuous improvement in your relationships doesn't happen by trying to change other people. Trying to do that will only frustrate everyone involved. The only part of any relationship you have the power to improve is the part you see when you look in the mirror.

THE PAINFUL ART OF SELF-IMPROVEMENT

Ashley recently talked me into buying some workout videos so that we could exercise together at home. Even though I have a hard time saying no to her, I was reluctant at first. I was picturing myself hopping around my living room in leg warmers like the people in my mom's 1980s workout videos, and it wasn't a pretty picture. I've never looked good in Spandex.

I finally came around and bought them (the videos, not the Spandex), but what really sold me was walking past the mirror one day with my shirt off and taking an honest self-assessment. I had to admit that I looked a whole lot more like a before picture than an after one! Looking at the guys on the cover of the video was proof that I had a lot of room for improvement. My passion for ice cream and Mexican food had put a lot of love into my love handles.

I try to stay healthy, but I'll probably never be able to see my abs. With all the feasting I read about in the Bible, I'm not sure you should ever trust a skinny Christian.

Working to improve our bodies definitely has some benefits, but working to improve our relationships has infinitely greater benefits. If we want to live a life of continuous improvement in our relationships, I believe we need to base the standard of love on the perfect example of Christ.

One of the behaviors perpetuating unhealthy relationships is the tendency to compare ourselves to other people who are doing worse than we are to give us a false sense of achievement. We presume that since our relationships aren't as bad as the ones we see on our favorite reality TV shows or our marriages look a lot better than the marriages of most of our relatives, then we must be doing okay.

> REAL IMPROVEMENT COMES WHEN WE'RE WILLING TO GET BRUTALLY HONEST WITH OUR SELF-ASSESSMENTS.

This mind-set keeps us trapped in a cycle of dysfunction. I could stay in poor physical shape if I made it my mission to find someone with a bigger gut and reassure myself that since I'm not as big as that guy, I must be doing fine. Real improvement comes when we're willing to get brutally honest with our self-assessments. Our comparisons should be with the best version of what we could become.

EMBRACING YOUR GOD-GIVEN DESIGN

Most nights, our kids' bedtime routine includes a story. My two older boys are pretty tough critics, and it's difficult to come up with something original night after night. If the story is "lame" or "boring," they're quick to tell me. You've got to have pretty thick skin to tell a story to Cooper and Connor.

I try to tell them stories with a moral to teach them a lesson about life and faith, because that's the way Jesus taught. It seems to have worked, because we're still telling his stories two thousand years later.

One story that seemed to get the boys thinking and hold their attention was the tale of "Doug the Slug."

I'd been having a conversation with my boys where they brought up things they didn't like about themselves and things they didn't like about each other. It hurt my heart to hear them talking like this, because as their dad, I want them to love themselves and love each other. Sadly, many of us never outgrow those insecurities about ourselves or prejudices about one another, so I told them this story:

There once was a slug named Doug. He wanted to be more like his friends Gary the Grasshopper, who could jump high, or Betty the Butterfly, who could fly and had beautiful colors, but Doug wasn't a butterfly or a grasshopper. Doug was a slug.

When Doug looked at himself, all he saw was slime. Slugs, after all, are pretty slimy. Doug was convinced that he would never accomplish much of anything because of how he was made. Sometimes other bugs would make fun of him for being so slimy, and he would hang his head low while they laughed.

One day, Doug heard his friends Gary the Grasshopper and Betty the Butterfly screaming for help. The giant spider who lived in their tree had caught them in his web, and he was walking toward them to eat them. They were so afraid. Doug was afraid, too, but he knew he had to do something to help his friends. He thought to himself, *I'm just a slimy slug. I can't do anything to help them!*

But then Doug thought of something he had never thought of before. He crawled as fast as he could go (which, for a slug, isn't very fast) to the spider web, and without thinking about his own safety, he bravely jumped on his friends and started covering them with his slime, which made them so slippery they were able to get free from the web! The spider angrily ran toward Doug, but the spider slipped on the slime and fell out of the tree all the way down to the ground below.

Doug the Slug became a hero! He had saved his friends. All the bugs who used to make fun of him started trying to hang out with him so they could get some of his famous slime on themselves. That day, for the first time, Doug realized he had been created for a purpose, and from then on, every time he looked down at his slime, he smiled.

The end.

God has created each of us to be a unique masterpiece, and he loves us (so we should love ourselves) just the way we are. The Bible says it this way: "For we are God's masterpiece. He has created us anew in Christ Jesus, so we can do the good things he planned for us long ago" (Eph. 2:10).

I want my kids to know that they're each a masterpiece. God created them exactly how they were meant to be. That doesn't mean they shouldn't strive for continuous improvement through all the seasons of their lives, but it does mean they're loved just the way they are. Completely and unconditionally.

I think we can all get caught up in a trap of comparing ourselves to others. It leads either to a false sense of pride when we feel superior to others or an unhealthy sense of insignificance when we feel we don't measure up to others. God looks at us through a different lens. He loves you and me exactly as we are, but he loves us too much to leave us exactly as we are. He wants us to become all we were created to be.

You need to know that you're loved completely and unconditionally. It doesn't matter where you've been or what you've done or what has been done to you. Your creator made you to be a masterpiece, and he loves you with an eternal love. His love gives you the ability to truly love yourself.

> YOUR CREATOR MADE YOU TO BE A MASTERPIECE, AND HE LOVES YOU WITH AN ETERNAL LOVE.

KNOWING WHO YOU ARE

The first step in genuinely loving yourself is to know who you are. I'm not talking about knowing your family history or your personality profile but having an understanding of your identity. This comes from knowing what God says about you.

There are many truths God wants you to know about yourself, but for the purposes of this chapter, I'd like to start with seven. If you will marinate on these promises from God, they can unlock the door to knowing yourself and loving yourself the way God desires for you to do.

1. You are loved.

One of the most mind-blowing realities the Bible teaches is that the God of the universe loves us. He loves you so much he sent his only son, Jesus, to rescue you and bring you home.

> "For this is how God loved the world: He gave his one and only Son, so that everyone who believes in him will not perish but have eternal life" (John 3:16).

2. You need Jesus.

He desires to be the Savior of your soul, the leader of your life, your guide, and your friend. Without him, your life will never be what God intended it to be. With him, you can experience all God has for you. Jesus did not come to make you religious; he came to make you alive!

> "Jesus told him, 'I am the way, the truth, and the life. No one can come to the Father except through me'" (John 14:6).

3. You are a part of God's master plan.

You are not on planet Earth by accident! The scientific and genetic odds against your birth are enormous, but you're here as part of God's plan. His will for your life is beautiful and unique.

> "'For I know the plans I have for you,' says the LORD. 'They are plans for good and not for disaster, to give you a future and a hope'" (Jer. 29:11).

4. You can be completely forgiven.

Once you trust Jesus for forgiveness, your sins are no longer counted against you, so don't live in regret. You are not defined by what you've done. God never measures our value by what we've done or by what's been done to us but by what he has done for us on the cross. God's grace takes away our sin and makes us a new creation, so we can live in freedom and peace.

"But if we confess our sins to him, he is faithful and just to forgive us our sins and to cleanse us from all wickedness" (1 John 1:9).

5. You are not alone.

We all have those moments when we feel lonely and abandoned, but even in your darkest hour, God is with you. He has never left your side, and he never will.

"For God has said, 'I will never fail you. I will never abandon you'" (Heb. 13:5b).

6. You are part of God's family.

Our faith in Christ brings us adoption into God's family. You are literally a son or daughter of God and an heir in his eternal kingdom.

"See how very much our Father loves us, for he calls us his children, and that is what we are!" (1 John 3:1a).

7. You have a home in heaven.

Jesus is preparing a place just for you. A perfect place awaits where the trouble and pain of this life will be no more, and you'll celebrate forever with your Savior and all of God's family.

"Don't let your hearts be troubled. Trust in God, and trust also in me. There is more than enough room in my Father's home. If this were not so, would I have told you that I am going to prepare a place for you? When everything is ready, I will come and get you, so that you will always be with me where I am" (John 14:1–3).

STOP OBSESSING ABOUT YOUR AGE

Our culture tends to define people in superficial ways, including wealth, appearance, and age. In recent years, there seems to be an even greater obsession with age.

When you're watching the news or reading a magazine story, it seems like one of the very first identifying marks we're told about a person is his or her age. Our culture seems to do a pretty good job of conditioning us from very early on to obsess about age. Cosmetic surgery is a multibillion dollar industry because we're all trying to rub on that Oil of Delay and hold onto youth.

We also seem to fall into the trap of comparing ourselves to others in what they had accomplished by our age to see if we're measuring up, and the deck always seems pretty stacked against us. As I write this, I am thirty-six years old. By age thirty-three, Thomas Jefferson had written the Declaration of Independence, Alexander the Great had conquered the known world, and my Savior, Jesus Christ, had saved the planet from their sins.

If I compared my meager accomplishments to those guys, I'd pretty much feel like a bum. Here's the good news: God's not nearly as interested in our ages as we seem to be.

When you read the Bible, you'll see that he's in the habit of using people the world calls too young or too old to change the planet. He used a hundred-year-old nomad named Abraham to start the nation of Israel. He chose an eighty-year-old murderer named Moses to lead Israel out of Egypt.

He chose an adolescent shepherd boy named David to take on a giant named Goliath, and he chose an unwed teenage girl named Mary to be the mother of the Messiah.

HERE'S THE GOOD NEWS: GOD'S NOT NEARLY AS INTERESTED IN OUR AGES AS WE SEEM TO BE.

If you feel too young or too old to change the world, remember that God doesn't exclusively use people with the right age or the right résumé. He uses people with the right heart.

Don't beat yourself up if you aren't where you'd hoped to be by this point in your life. God is just getting started with you! His plan for you is an eternal one (and eternity is a really long time). Keep trusting him, seeking him, and being faithful to make the most of your current situation, and one day you'll see that you've accomplished far more for his glory and the world's good than you could have ever realized.

TRUST GOD, NOT YOUR FEELINGS

Sometimes our feelings get in the way of love. Whenever we find ourselves in a place where our feelings are incompatible with God's truth, we've got to trust God over our feelings. This is especially important when it comes to understanding our own identities. We can't look within ourselves to discover who we are; we can only look to the one who created us.

The Bible tells us the story of a man who struggled with

this issue of identity. His name was Gideon. He lived in a time of chaos and uncertainty. Israel had been invaded by an army of brutal oppressors, and the people of Israel were living in terror.

When we're introduced to Gideon, he's hiding in a cave, threshing wheat in a winepress. He's doing whatever he can do to stay alive, but it's clear that he's terrified and confused. God sends an angel to remind Gideon who he is. The angel shows up and greets Gideon by saying, "Mighty hero, the LORD is with you!" (Judg. 6:12).

Gideon was probably left scratching his head, thinking the angel must have been talking to somebody else. Gideon didn't look like a mighty hero. We get the picture that he was pretty scrawny. He probably didn't eat much protein powder or spend a lot of time in the weight room. All he saw when he looked in the mirror was a skinny dude hiding in a cave.

I'm not sure if you've noticed, but our world seems pretty obsessed with status, titles, and labels. We often try to categorize and define other people by labels, such as ethnicity, occupation, net worth, height, weight, age, academic pedigree, salary, job title, and the list goes on. If we're not careful, we can start basing our identities on such labels.

THE TROUBLE WITH BASING YOUR IDENTITY ON LABELS IS THAT THERE'S NO MAN-MADE LABEL WITH THE POWER TO DEFINE YOUR SOUL.

The trouble with basing your identity on labels is that there's no man-made label with the power to define your soul. God is the one who created you, and he alone has the right to tell you who you really are. Once you find your significance in him, everything else comes into focus.

Gideon questioned the angel's message because Gideon had

assumed that if God was as powerful as he claimed to be, he wouldn't have allowed Gideon and his people to live in fear and chaos. Gideon had to wrestle with his faith before he could embrace his identity.

Maybe you've had a difficult time trusting God for the same factors Gideon wrestled to understand. Perhaps you look at the heartbreak in your life and think to yourself, *Well, if there's really a God, then I guess he's either too weak to change my situation or he's too indifferent to care.*

The truth is that God is right by your side, just like he was right there with Gideon. God had allowed the situation to get bleak before he intervened. Sometimes God will do that in your life too. I believe God often lets a situation get worse just to make room for a bigger miracle.

Gideon eventually did prove to be the mighty warrior God knew he was all along. God looks at you, and he says you are a masterpiece. He says you are a new creation in Christ. He says you are his child. He says you are loved. Don't let the labels of this world stick to you. God has labeled you as loved, and his opinion of you is the only one that counts.

GOD'S WILL FOR YOUR LIFE

Maybe you're thinking you'd have the courage to be a warrior like Gideon if you had the clarity Gideon was given about God's will for his life. Even my friends who don't have much faith have asked, "What's God's will for my life?"

In one way or another, I believe that's a question we've all wrestled with. The Bible says that we're born with this sense of eternity or destiny in our hearts, but for most of us, we have a hard time discovering what that looks like. I don't think our loving creator intended for this whole process to confuse us, because the Bible gives us some pretty clear steps for discovering God's will.

Step 1: Start by doing the stuff you already know is God's will for your life.

The Bible clearly gives us some basics to help us get started. It's clear that God's plan for your life begins with a relationship with him. I'm not talking about religion or rules; I'm talking about knowing him and loving him, which is made possible by what Jesus did on the cross. Once we begin that relationship, God's will for us includes praying, being thankful, loving other people, serving, caring, giving, and using his personalized one-thousand-page text message to us (the Bible) as our standard for living.

Step 2: Discover how your unique design reveals your destiny.

I believe we discover our unique callings when we find places where our God-given abilities and our God-given passions intersect at a point of need in the world. When we're living out our destinies, we make the world a better place and find deep fulfillment all at the same time. We can accomplish this through our vocations, but these dreams are often accomplished through service outside of our vocations.

Step 3: Get started right where you are.

The biggest mistake we make in searching for God's will is waiting for conditions to become perfect before we actually start doing something. If you wait for perfection, you'll be waiting forever. Right where you are, in your school, in your job, in your neighborhood, in your home, God has already put world-changing opportunities all around you. Ask him to help you see those opportunities more clearly and then get going. He didn't create you to sit on the sidelines; he made you to change the world!

BROKEN PIECES

We all want to be the best we can be, but a factor that often holds people back from loving themselves is the nagging disappointment of how life has turned out so far. Many of us start out wide-eyed and optimistic that our dreams will come true. We paint a picture of life filled with success and happiness.

Reality in adulthood rarely measures up to the idealized dreams we had in childhood. As a kid, I had plans to be a professional athlete, a billionaire, and president of the United States. So far, none of those has happened. Instead of dwelling on how I've failed to live up to my childhood fantasies, I am learning to look at the picture God is painting with my life. It may not look like what I had in my head, but in light of eternity, the picture God is painting is something far more meaningful.

A few years ago, my perspective on this changed in a single night. It all began with a trip to Walmart. God definitely has a sense of humor. Only he could bring a life-changing moment out of a trip to Walmart.

Our family was preparing for the Christmas season, and we were loading up on our usual groceries while simultaneously trying to distract our kids from all the breakable items. Several months earlier, one of our kids had knocked over an end-of-aisle

THE SEVEN LAWS OF LOVE

wine display leaving broken glass and red wine spilled all over the floor. I had been attempting to avoid contact with all Walmart employees ever since. I strongly believed they had a picture of our family on the "Most Wanted Criminals" board in the employee break room.

On this day, we managed not to break anything, but we did end up buying more than I was planning to buy. That seems to happen every time for some reason. One of the unexpected purchases came when we passed a display of gingerbread house kits.

My kids immediately started their begging. Normally, I have the strength to resist their pleas because if they had their way, the cart would be filled to the brim with Twinkies and toys. This request caught my attention because as I looked at the box, I envisioned a magical evening.

My mind created a scene from a Charles Dickens novel as our family cheerfully assembled and decorated the gingerbread house. There would be Christmas music playing in the background and eggnog and good cheer. At some point, one of my children would say with Tiny Tim's British accent, "God bless us, every one!"

We bought the kit, but on the way home, the boys started fighting over the box. We weren't setting the tone for the magical Christmas evening I'd envisioned. I loudly threatened to pull the minivan over on several occasions during the short drive home. Visions of sugarplums were no longer dancing through my head.

When we arrived at the house and emptied the contents of the box, the pieces of the gingerbread house were all broken. I was so disappointed. I had just wasted eight dollars. That's a lot of money for gingerbread. After expressing my frustration with the kids, I started pouting like a spoiled toddler.

Ashley is so much more patient than I am. She came over to me and asked what was wrong. I thought the answer was pretty obvious, but I tried not to sound condescending in my response. "It's broken! It's ruined."

She smiled and gently replied, "It's not ruined."

I looked at her like she was crazy, and in frustration I held up the box and replied, "Of course it's ruined! It's never going to look like the picture on the box."

What she said next completely changed my thinking. In her patience and wisdom, she was about to teach me a lesson much more valuable than my eight-dollar purchase. She said, "It doesn't have to look like the picture on the box."

Think about that statement. So much of my frustration in life comes from unmet expectations. I'll bet it's the same in your life too. I paint a picture in my mind of how a situation should play out, and if the end result doesn't look exactly like my mental masterpiece, then I walk away disappointed. But imagine what could happen if we allow God to create a masterpiece even with the broken pieces of our hearts and lives.

IMAGINE WHAT COULD HAPPEN IF WE ALLOW GOD TO CREATE A MASTERPIECE EVEN WITH THE BROKEN PIECES OF OUR HEARTS AND LIVES.

Our family went to work that night, and we had a ball with those broken pieces. We didn't end up with an actual gingerbread house, but we had some amazing, oddly-shaped gingerbread cookies. They were delicious.

We laughed more that night than we had in a long time. We were covered in icing and crumbs by the end of it, but it was well worth the mess. I almost missed out on that moment because the rigidity of my expectations didn't make room for the beautiful spontaneity of the opportunity. I'm so thankful my wife had more vision than I had.

Not only did my family enjoy an unexpected blessing with those broken pieces, but many other families were blessed as well. A few weeks later, I was preaching a Christmas message at church, and I shared this story. So many families struggle during the holidays because it's a time of year that can amplify our disappointments.

When our lives or our families don't look like the picture-perfect images we imagined, we can be faced with weighty sadness and self-defeat. I shared the lesson I'd learned with the broken pieces of the gingerbread house and reassured the congregation. "Maybe your family doesn't look anything like the perfect picture on the box, but it doesn't have to! God loves you right where you are. He's the only perfect part of our lives, and he wants to create something beautiful with the broken pieces of your hearts, your families, and your lives, if you let him."

Of all the stories I shared that December, the broken pieces of the gingerbread house resonated more than any other. Countless families came up to me afterward and said, "You were describing our home. You were describing our family. The holidays are a painful reminder of our brokenness, but now they'll be a beautiful reminder of God's love for us and the masterpiece he can create with our broken pieces."

I almost missed this beautiful blessing because of my stubbornness, pride, and lack of vision. Don't miss the opportunities God has for your life. Don't overlook the blessings hidden in the broken pieces.

Maybe your life doesn't look like the picture on the box right now. Perhaps you struggle with deep disappointment over the way your life and your relationships have developed up to this point in your story. Whatever your current circumstances may be, I challenge you to look at your life through the lens of God's love for you. His love for you is limitless, and his plans for you are perfect.

Above all else, remember that God loves you. Your identity isn't wrapped up in your net worth or your résumé. You are loved completely and unconditionally by your creator, and his love empowers you to love yourself and everyone else. God loves you, and God is never wrong. Have the faith to trust him and love yourself.

> ABOVE ALL ELSE, REMEMBER THAT GOD LOVES YOU. YOUR IDENTITY ISN'T WRAPPED UP IN YOUR NET WORTH OR YOUR RÉSUMÉ.

DISCUSSION QUESTIONS

1. What's one thing you would change about yourself if you could?
2. What's one thing you think God might want to change about you?
3. What do you believe is the difference between a healthy self-confidence and selfish pride?
4. How would your life look different if you could replace all your insecurities with complete security in your identity? What's holding you back from doing it?

CHAPTER 14

LOVING YOUR CREATOR

Jesus replied, "You must love the LORD your God with all your heart, all your soul, and all your mind." This is the first and greatest commandment.

—MATTHEW 22:37–38

When my oldest son, Cooper, was born, somebody gave us a DVD of baby sign language that we started showing him when he was just a few months old. As new parents, we had no idea what we were doing, but we thought if our baby learned sign language, then everybody would think we really knew our stuff.

The DVD didn't make him a fluent phenomenon in signing, but it turned out there was one sign that he picked up and consistently used. He knew what it meant, and he used it often. It was the sign for the word *more*. Before he could speak a word, he had already discovered the instinctive human fascination with more.

As a baby, you just want more milk or more toys, but as we

grow, the hunger for "more" grows. In adulthood, most of us are fueled by the drive for more money, more success, more pleasure, more fun, more rest, more sex, and more of pretty much everything else. Our materialistic, hedonistic culture convinces us that we're not happy, but if we just buy a little more of a certain product, then maybe we will be. It's a vicious cycle that never ends until we discover the truth in God's Word.

It reminds me of the racing greyhounds at the dog track near our old home in Florida. Those dogs spent their whole lives running in a circle chasing a mechanical rabbit. If a dog was ever fast enough to actually catch the mechanical rabbit, he would never run again. He would have attained his life's pursuit only to discover the painful truth that he'd been chasing a lie.

Here's the truth: More stuff will never make you happy. It's a myth. It's an empty pursuit. Contentment isn't a result of having more; it's a result of wanting less. Don't spend your life running in a circle in pursuit of more money, more prestige, or more comfort. Until you're content with what you've already got, you won't be content no matter how much you get.

> CONTENTMENT ISN'T A RESULT OF HAVING MORE; IT'S A RESULT OF WANTING LESS.

God wants you to live in a spirit of gratitude and contentment. Don't let the selfishness of this world rob you of that. Choose to give thanks in all circumstances and be truly content with what you already have, and the "more" that comes your way will just be the icing on the cake. God has many blessings in store for you, but you won't be able to fully embrace them until you're willing to trade more of this world for more of God.

God will often ask us to let go of things so our hands and hearts will be open to the greater gifts he wants to place there.

Sometimes he asks us to let go simply because we're holding on too tightly to the stuff of this world and loving them more than we're loving God. Anything we love more than God is an idol, and idolatry is the enemy of genuine love.

Jesus had an encounter with a rich, young ruler where this truth was displayed in a dramatic way. This rich, young guy seemed to have the whole world going for him, and he came to Jesus asking what he needed to do to inherit eternal life. Jesus told him to obey all the commandments, and the young man replied that he had.

What happened next was shocking. Jesus looked at this young man with love and compassion, and he knew that there was a love for fame and fortune in his heart that surpassed his love for God. Jesus gave him an eternity-defining choice by saying, "There's still one thing you lack. Go and sell everything you have and give the money to the poor, and you'll have treasure in heaven. Then, come follow me."

In essence, Jesus was saying, "Get rid of all those distractions. It's holding you back from experiencing real love and real life. I want to give you treasure that will last for eternity, but you've got to be willing to trust me enough to let go of all your stuff."

The young man walked away sad. He chose his stuff over his Savior. He chose the world's way over God's way. He missed out on the adventure he was born to live. When he was forced to choose between the two, he wanted more gold instead of more God.

If we place greater value on any relationship or possession than on our love for God, then we're guilty of idolatry. We can't just love God a little bit. We have to love him wholeheartedly. He deserves nothing less.

THE FIRST STEP TO LOVING GOD

Our love for God requires our trust in God and our obedience to God. We can't say we love God but then disregard his instructions. Very often, our selfish human nature can be in constant conflict with God's will for us.

This tug-of-war between my selfishness and my conscience happens more than I'd like to admit. There have been so many times my selfish side won out, and I completely and willfully ignored an opportunity for a life-changing moment. There have been other times when I swallowed my pride and said yes to God. Those are the moments that have become turning points in my life and have taught me a life-changing principle: God will never ask you to let go of anything unless he intends to replace it with something better.

GOD WILL NEVER ASK YOU TO LET GO OF ANYTHING UNLESS HE INTENDS TO REPLACE IT WITH SOMETHING BETTER.

As a quick disclaimer, this principle does not mean God is going to tell you to give up your spouse or your kids so you can replace them with somebody "better." You've got to be permanently committed to your faith and your family, but anything or anyone else in your life might be something God will eventually ask you to cut loose.

I experienced a dramatic example of this a few years ago when my family was preparing to move from Florida back to our home in Georgia. I was having breakfast with a pastor in town named Andre. I loved hanging out with Pastor Andre for several reasons. First off, he was South African, so he had a super-cool accent. Almost everything he said sounded sophisticated. I grew up in Kentucky, so my accent, by contrast, is the opposite of cool and sophisticated. I was hoping that just by associating with Andre, people might start assuming that I was cool too.

As much as I loved the accent, that wasn't the real reason I loved hanging out with him. Andre had an inspiring and contagious passion for helping the homeless community in our area. As he would talk about Jesus' teachings and how we are all called to help the least of these, he would beam with energy and vision. He was putting his faith into action, and it challenged me to do the same. After a cup of coffee and conversation with Andre, I always felt like my body and my soul had both just received a jolt of caffeine.

As we were sitting at Panera and I was munching on a bagel, I asked Andre what his outreach ministry needed at the moment. I was really just making conversation; I didn't actually believe I would be able to do much to help. Andre said, "Our biggest need right now is transportation for these men and women. They have places to go like job training and addiction recovery programs, but they don't have a way to get there. If we had a van, we could take them to these places and open up a new world for them."

At the time we had a van. It was actually our primary vehicle, even though it was pretty beat up. I had bought it for a couple thousand bucks on Craigslist, and it had always had engine trouble plus this strange lasagna-like smell that we could never cover up no matter how much Lysol we sprayed in the van. On top of that, my rambunctious kids had added a bunch of new stains and smells of their own. The car was on its last leg. Even my mechanic told me it was on death's door.

The van wasn't much, but I still had no interest in giving it away. I mean, it might have smelled like old lasagna, but it was still running. I could get something for it. And besides all that, I'm cheap! That's why I bought an old van in the first place.

God knows I'm cheap. He made me this way. Surely someone else could give Andre's ministry a van. But then I reminded myself that we can't show our love to God without giving him our trust and our obedience. To show distrust or disobedience to God is to take our love away from him.

> TO SHOW DISTRUST OR DISOBEDIENCE TO GOD IS TO TAKE OUR LOVE AWAY FROM HIM.

I was having this argument with myself in my mind while Andre continued on with his world-changing plea in that beautiful accent, and finally I blurted out what I should have said right from the beginning: "I think God wants me to give you my van. I want to give you my van."

Andre was elated. I was terrified. I knew I had done exactly what God wanted me to do, and I knew that God always takes care of his kids and we can always trust him, and yet, the selfish part of me wondered if I had just made a huge mistake.

Fast-forward a few weeks. My family was back in Georgia and recovering from the emotional and physical trauma that results from an interstate move with small kids in tow. We had sold our remaining car to free up some cash until we closed on our house, so for the first time in our marriage, we didn't own a vehicle. I was borrowing a car from my parents.

There were many moments during those trying weeks of transition, while we were sleeping on air mattresses and driving around in a crowded, borrowed car, when I silently vented my frustration to God. I remember thinking, *Lord, why on earth did you have me give that van away? We don't have anything to replace it! Was that really you speaking to me, or was it just the burrito I ate the night before?*

It was during one of these venting moments that my phone rang. It was a guy from church named Gary. I didn't know Gary and his wife, Sue, very well at the time, but they were about to change our lives and begin a friendship that would become a permanent source of encouragement.

Gary started off, saying, "Look, I know this might sound pretty crazy. It actually sounds pretty crazy to me. I mean, I've never done anything like this before, but I heard your family doesn't have a vehicle currently, and I feel strongly that God is telling me to buy you a brand-new van."

A new van! I didn't even know they came new. I had been buying used junkers for so long that I didn't even know new ones were an option!

My mouth was hanging open like I had just seen a spaceship with Elvis Presley waving from a window. I was stunned, speechless. It felt like God was winking at me and reminding me of that beautiful truth: *he will never take anything from you unless he intends to replace it with something better.*

> IN YOUR LIFE, WHENEVER YOU LOSE A JOB, AN INVESTMENT, OR EVEN A RELATIONSHIP, TRUST THAT GOD WILL FILL THAT EMPTY SPACE WITH A GREAT BLESSING.

In your life, whenever you lose a job, an investment, or even a relationship, trust that God will fill that empty space with a great blessing. It won't always be something you can measure with monetary value, but life's greatest gifts can't be bought or sold. The bottom line is this: God is for you, he loves you, and his plans for your life are even better than your own plans. The first step in loving God is simply trusting God.

TRUSTING GOD WHEN YOU CAN'T SEE THE BIG PICTURE

I was a child of the 1980s. I'll bet you're already getting flashbacks of leg warmers, Cabbage Patch Kids, and big hair. It was quite a decade. I grew up on movies like *Back to the Future, Top Gun, The Goonies,* and my personal favorite . . . *The Karate Kid*!

If you've never seen *The Karate Kid*, the plot follows a teenage kid named Daniel who wants to learn karate so he can defend himself from local bullies. He meets a mysterious older man named Mr. Miyagi who turns out to be a karate master. They form a friendship, and Daniel eventually begs Mr. Miyagi to teach him karate. Mr. Miyagi agrees, on the condition that Daniel follow instructions no matter what. No questions asked.

Daniel agrees and shows up for his first day of lessons, but instead of teaching him karate, Mr. Miyagi tells him to wax all of his cars. Daniel has to do it with a very specific circular motion to put the wax on with one hand and take it off with the other. By the end of the day, Daniel's arms and shoulders are hurting badly, but he doesn't complain. He shows up the next morning certain that this will be the day he finally learns karate, but instead, Mr. Miyagi tells him to paint the fence. He has to paint it with a specific motion of moving his hands up and down in a continuous motion so there aren't any streaks in the paint.

After several days of forced labor, Daniel finally snaps. He confronts his teacher and accuses him of making him a slave instead of teaching him karate. Mr. Miyagi says, "I have been teaching you karate this entire time. Show me how to wax the car. Show me how to paint the fence."

As Daniel begins to mimic the motions from those tasks, Mr. Miyagi begins to throw a flurry of punches and kicks at Daniel, which, to Daniel's amazement, he is able to block. Daniel's body had been learning karate even though Daniel didn't realize it. Mr. Miyagi bows to his student, and in that moment something clicked in my head. For me, that wasn't just a moment of Hollywood magic; it was a moment where some truths of God's Word came to life in real and practical ways.

> YOU'RE ON YOUR WAY TO BECOMING A SPIRITUAL BLACK BELT, AND YOUR HEAVENLY FATHER IS WITH YOU EVERY STEP OF THE WAY.

So many times in my life, I feel that I'm begging God to reveal his will and that all I'm doing is toiling away at some mundane, repetitive task just waiting for my life to begin. What I've come to realize is that God doesn't waste anything. He's always teaching us, always shaping us. He's preparing us to respond instinctively to the battles of life with a level of faith and skill we didn't know we possessed. You're on your way to becoming a spiritual black belt, and your heavenly Father is with you every step of the way.

WHEN WE DON'T TRUST GOD

Some people carry a deep-seated, unspoken distrust of God. We look at the tragedy and pain of our lives, and our wounded faith hinders our ability to fully love. It makes life feel like a prison instead of a gift. Pain has a way of blinding us to the bigger picture.

April 16, 2007, was an infamous day in American history. I remember it vividly. All day long the news stations streamed coverage of the worst school shooting we'd seen in the United States in ages. A student at Virginia Tech had gone on a shooting spree. Seemingly without any motive, this troubled young man opened fire on his classmates and professors. In minutes, lives were lost and the nation was gripped with grief. Millions stayed glued to their televisions watching the drama unfold.

As the day went on, commentators and on-the-street interviewees asked, "Where is God? If there is a good and loving God, how could he allow this to happen?"

I suppose it's natural to ask questions like that in moments of tragedy. In our pain, we falsely assume that God is absent or God doesn't care.

I had a unique vantage point as the nation mourned that day. I was watching the drama unfold from a hospital room where Ashley would eventually give birth to our second son, Connor. As most of the nation watched the tragedy of death, I witnessed the miracle of new life.

That's often how God seems to work. In our pain, we might shake our fists at heaven and wonder where God is hiding, but God is always working. He's always weaving stories together for our good and his glory.

One beautiful day, he will set all things right and make all things new. We will finally see the big picture. We will understand how all the circumstances fit together and how he was with us and for us in every moment. In the meantime, we must choose to trust him. That's the essence of faith.

Faith is a choice, not a feeling. It means choosing to trust God even when life doesn't seem to make sense.

A limited trust in God will limit your ability to love. You can't wait for your circumstances to improve before you choose to trust him. God will usually change your perspective before he will change your circumstances. Choose to have faith, and you'll instantly open the door for more peace and love to flow into your life.

GOD WILL USUALLY CHANGE YOUR PERSPECTIVE BEFORE HE WILL CHANGE YOUR CIRCUMSTANCES.

The more you trust God, the more you'll love God. The more you love God, the more capacity you'll have to love yourself and everyone else.

Even when life doesn't seem to make sense, make the choice to trust God. You don't have to figure out everything. In fact, the Bible never once says, "Thou shalt figure it out," but over and over it says, "Trust God." He's the one who has it all figured out.

THE HEART OF WORSHIP

God never wants us just going through the motions in our relationship with him. He doesn't want our coldhearted servitude; he wants us. He wants a real relationship, which is something so much more than mere religion. Our worship of him flows from our love for him, and we can't truly love him until we invest the time to know him.

Have you ever been to a restaurant to celebrate somebody's birthday? For me, one of the most painfully awkward experiences on earth is the moment when your server tries to recruit a bunch of fellow servers to gather around your table and force some false enthusiasm as they sing a birthday song. It creates a pretty funny contrast. In my family, we wildly, passionately, and joyfully sing (usually off-key) at the top of our lungs to honor the birthday boy or girl while flanked by servers singing the same song to the same person but without any heart or passion.

I think most churches are full of people who sing songs to God with the halfhearted enthusiasm of the singing servers at a typical restaurant. There is no joy because they are singing to a stranger. They're singing to someone they don't know in the hopes that maybe they'll get a tip (or some kind of blessing) as a result of carrying out their duty.

Nobody (including God) enjoys that kind of worship. God is looking for loving family members to sit around the table with him, laughing and learning and singing and feasting and just enjoying his company. He wants to give you much more than a tip. He wants to give you a relationship, not a religion. He wants your worship to flow from your love for him. He wants you to inherit the keys to his kingdom.

Out of this kind of relationship, you'll begin to discover that every part of your life can be an act of worship. Connecting with God is not confined to Sunday mornings. He can be a constant presence in your life, and as you grow in your love for him, your life (and your songs) will develop an intimate sense of love, passion, and joy for God.

GOD'S TEAM

I live in the South, where college football is practically a religion for a lot of folks. People look forward to Saturdays when the tailgating and trash-talking leads up to a battle on the field, and if your team wins, then you're going to have bragging rights in the office on Monday!

We were living in Florida when some good folks at our church gave us tickets to the Florida Gators game against the Kentucky Wildcats. Since I'm a Kentucky grad, they knew I'd be interested in the tickets. Even though UK is more of a basketball school, I still cheer for my Wildcats all football season long (even when they're getting beat by every other team in the SEC).

This was a big family moment for us because our two young sons had never been to a college football game. We let them pick out whatever they wanted to wear, and because their team loyalty hadn't really set in yet, they chose outfits that really confused me. They wanted to wear Kentucky jerseys and Florida Gator hats. They wanted to cheer for both teams.

I didn't take the time to explain to them that this was crazy because we were already running late. Once we got to "The Swamp" in Gainesville, Florida, and started weaving our way through drunk college students to get to the stadium, people started noticing my kids' creative wardrobe choice and then looked at me like I was committing some form of child abuse. Few things will confuse an intoxicated football fan like seeing somebody cheering for both teams.

As the night went on and my boys saw that everybody there was cheering for one team or the other, I explained that in life we need to know which team we're on. We have to commit to a team or else the game is pointless.

In the scope of eternity, which team you like on Saturdays won't make that much of a difference, but when it comes to our allegiance to God, we have to be all in. We can't wear a jersey that says, "I'm committed to you," but then wear a hat that shouts, "I'm not committed to you."

That kind of inconsistency only confuses the people around us and causes us to live with a schizophrenic sense of loyalty. To love God the way he demands and deserves, we must give our undivided loyalty. We must love what God loves and hate what God hates.

HATING WHAT GOD HATES

The Bible clearly teaches that God not only does love; God *is* love. We often assume that a loving God doesn't hate anything, but the truth is, because God loves us so much, he hates anything that could harm us. For example, God created the gift of marriage, so the Bible teaches that God hates divorce. God obviously loves divorced people, but his heart breaks when marriages end that way. He wants more for us.

WHEN WE LEARN WHAT GOD HATES, WE ARE ABLE TO SEE MORE CLEARLY THE BLESSINGS AND THE POTENTIAL PITFALLS THAT ARE BEFORE US.

When we learn what God hates, we are able to see more clearly the blessings and the potential pitfalls that are before us. You may think any mention of hate is out of place in a book about love, but I believe understanding one helps us understand the other. We can love God most perfectly when we gain a better understanding of both what he loves and what he hates. The Bible deals with these issues in the book of Proverbs.

> There are six things the LORD hates,
> seven that are detestable to him:
>> haughty eyes,
>> a lying tongue,
>> hands that shed innocent blood,
>> a heart that devises wicked schemes,
>> feet that are quick to rush into evil,
>> a false witness who pours out lies
>> and a person who stirs up conflict in the community.
>
> (PROV. 6:16–19 NIV)

221

Let's unpack these one at a time:

1. Pride

"Haughty eyes" refers to the sin of pride. God loves all people, so when we look down on others, it does harm to them and it does harm to us. Pride is pure selfishness. It is the sin that got Satan kicked out of heaven. Pride is the soil in which all other sin takes root.

2. Lying

"A lying tongue" refers to all lying in every form. Jesus is the truth, while Satan is the "father of lies." Truth and love are the cornerstones of God's character, so anything that is the enemy of truth is the enemy of God.

3. Unprovoked Violence

"Hands that shed innocent blood" refers to all forms of attack (whether physical, verbal, or psychological) motivated by selfishness. This behavior is the opposite of being a peacemaker, which is what God calls us to be.

4. Impure Motives

"A heart that devises wicked schemes" refers to all dark and secret motives that lead a person toward sin. God isn't concerned with outward appearances. He wants us to have pure hearts and pure motives.

5. Rebellion

"Feet that are quick to rush into evil" refers to rebellion against God's perfect law. Those who defiantly choose a path of lawlessness choose to make themselves enemies of God. Despite our defiant sin, we can turn back to God (repent) and be received with open arms because of his amazing grace.

6. Deception

"A false witness who pours out lies" refers to anyone who would deceive, pervert, or misrepresent the truth to deny justice. God's love for truth and justice brings disdain for dishonesty and injustice. Lovers of God must strive to bring justice to all people, especially to the victimized and marginalized.

7. Dissension

"A person who stirs up conflict in the community" refers to anyone who becomes a threat to unity and peace. This one is listed last to give it special attention, because God deeply desires a unified spirit of peace within his family (the church). There is power in unity and destruction in dissension. That doesn't mean we always agree, but it does mean that we work diligently to maintain what the Bible refers to as "the unity of the Spirit through the bond of peace" (Eph. 4:3 NIV).

HE LOVED YOU FIRST

The only reason we have the capability to love God (or anyone else) is that God loved us first. His love gives us the ability to give and receive love. Sometimes we have a difficult time loving God because we haven't grasped the security we should have from his love. We think it's something we have to earn instead of a gift he freely gives us.

Our perspectives change when we have children.

Our three-year-old son, Chandler, loves to cuddle. If cuddling were an Olympic sport, Chandler would be on the cover of a Wheaties box! One of his favorite pastimes is to be engulfed in what our family affectionately refers to as a "Chanwich." This happens when Ashley and I sandwich him with snuggles at the same time. He giggles and flashes his big, toothy grin as he pulls us both close to him at the same time while shouting the word, "Chanwich!"

Before my baby boy did a thing to earn my adoration, I already loved him with an unconditional love that only a parent can understand. When I hold him in my arms, I get a glimpse of the love our heavenly Father has for us. I'm just an imperfect human father, so multiply my love by infinity, and you'll see what God wants for his children.

ONE OF THE GREAT IRONIES OF LOVE IS THAT THE MORE WE MATURE IN OUR LOVE FOR GOD, THE MORE CHILDLIKE WE WILL BECOME.

I've learned so much about love simply by interacting with my kids. Children aren't preoccupied with social etiquette or anything that might hinder the enjoyment of love in its purest form. God put unblemished love within the hearts of children. It's important to apply grown-up experience and wisdom to these concepts, but we should never lose the wonder of a child.

One of the great ironies of love is that the more we mature in our love for God, the more childlike we will become. We will also become more confident, because we'll know our identity is based not on our appearances or performances, but in our eternal place in God's family.

PUTTING YOUR LOVE FOR GOD IN ACTION

Loving God shouldn't just make our own lives better; it should make the world around us better as a result. The more you love God, the more capacity you will have to love others. A love for God brings both peace and a burden to your heart to help others.

There are so many people in the world desperate for love. It's hard to watch the evening news or scroll through what's trending on the Internet without seeing a story of crisis and heartbreak. The technology used to deliver these stories is new, but the desperate need for love has been around forever. Each generation has unique opportunities to respond to unspeakable tragedy and evil with courageous love.

I visited the Holocaust Museum in Washington, DC, a few years ago, and the experience left a lasting impression. I saw pictures of the men, women, and children who were slaughtered in concentration camps. I saw evidence of genocide and some of the worst evils our world has ever seen. It was heartbreaking, and yet, there were triumphant stories of courage and self-sacrifice as well.

I stood at the exhibit honoring Oskar Schindler, a prominent German businessman who risked his life and gave up his fortune to save as many Jews as possible. The film *Schindler's List* poignantly captures the story of this unlikely hero. It is a touching tribute to the true heroes of the Holocaust.

Schindler had been a shrewd businessman and selfish womanizer leading up to the war, but seeing the travesties of the concentration camps eventually pierced Schindler's hard heart, and his cynicism was replaced with compassion. That compassion took root and created conviction. Schindler rightly recognized that he couldn't passively stand on the sidelines while people were being murdered. He had to take action.

He set up a phony operation in one of his factories and spent his money to hire Jews. He bribed guards and politicians to release the prisoners from the camps into his employment. He created a list with the names of every man, woman, and child he was in a position to rescue, and he spent all he had to rescue them.

The end of the film records a moment that allegedly occurred in real life. As Schindler prepared to leave Germany at the end of the war, he was surrounded by the more than one thousand people he saved.

With tears in his eyes, he looked at his gold ring and said, "This could have saved another person. I could have rescued one more person for this ring."

He looked at the car that was waiting to drive him away, and he cried, "Why did I keep this car? I could have sold it and saved another person."

One of his Jewish friends stepped forward to console him. He grabbed his shoulders and said, "Look at the lives you saved. There will be generations because of what you did."

I love that scene, because it reminds us of what is truly important. In the end, it won't matter how much money we have or the possessions we've collected. All that will matter is the love we've given to God and those around us and how we used our talents and resources to help others.

A LIFE OF LOVE IS A LIFE THAT IMPACTS ETERNITY.

A life of love is a life that impacts eternity. Imagine how your life and the world around you would look different if you leveraged all you had for love. God wants to change the world in you and through you. What are you waiting for?

DISCUSSION QUESTIONS

1. Who is a person in your life who seems to have a contagious love for God? What is it about that person's faith that is so inspiring?
2. How would your life look different if you made every decision to show honor and love for God?
3. What's one practical way you could display more love for God and for others?
4. How could you change the world through love? What's holding you back from doing it?

AFTERWORD
What's Next?

Do everything with love.

—1 CORINTHIANS 16:14

If you're like me, once you finish a book, you probably put it down and don't think much more about it. Maybe a couple stories or principles might stick in your head, but there's rarely a lasting impact. If you really liked the book, you might tell some people about it or post a review online, but that's usually the end of it.

I'm hoping that this book has left you wanting to take a next step. I'm grateful if you tell your friends about the book or write a review, but those are definitely not the most important steps you could take. Rather, I want you to do something that could have a life-changing impact for you. I want you to experience a positive revolution in your relationships.

The principles you've just read will have the greatest possibility of making a lasting difference in your relationships if you apply them immediately. I challenge you to begin with identifying one relationship you'd like to improve. Perhaps it is with your spouse, or a child, or a coworker, or a friend. Maybe it's already a healthy relationship, or perhaps it's broken. If someone isn't jumping to the forefront of your mind immediately, take a minute to ponder and pray about it.

Once a name emerges, commit to God and to yourself that you're going to reach out to that person with love by applying each of the Seven Laws of Love to the relationship in these specific ways:

1. Love requires commitment: Communicate your commitment to this person. Do it with your words and your actions. If you chose your spouse, it could be a vow renewal. If you chose a friend, it can start with something as simple as a text message saying something like, "I just wanted you to know I'm so thankful for you. So glad you're in my life. I'm here for you if you need anything at all. Ever!"

2. Love speaks truth: Confess to this person any deceit you've brought to the relationship. Even if there's been no deceit, increase the level and depth of honesty in the relationship by sharing something you've never told that person before. Unfiltered honesty will create deeper intimacy.

3. Love conquers fear: Think of an experience that potentially terrifies you. Maybe it's skydiving or something as simple as donating blood. Ask this person to come do it with you, and say, "I'm scared to do this, but if you're there, too, I know I can get through it."

4. Love offers grace: Confess any sin you committed against

this person; humbly ask his or her forgiveness and request the opportunity to rebuild trust. If this person has sinned against you, reach out and humbly offer your forgiveness.

5. Love selflessly sacrifices: Do an act of selfless service for this person. Do something thoughtful and unexpected that would make a big difference in his or her life, and do it with no expectation of repayment.

6. Love brings healing: Think of a place where this person has been wounded financially, emotionally, physically, or relationally, and commit to doing something specific to help promote healing.

7. Love lives forever: Recognize that each of these simple acts of love can have an eternal impact. Once you've completed the exercise of applying all Seven Laws in this single relationship, challenge the other person to choose one person and carry out these same acts of love. In addition to an ongoing relationship with this person you've chosen, you should also choose someone new and begin the process all over. In this way, you're creating a ripple effect of love that can touch many people and change the world in the process.

FINAL INSTRUCTIONS

A few years ago, I received a message from God in a very unlikely way. This two-word message gave me hope, and I pray it does the same for you.

I had just moved my family to a new city and was serving as a pastor in a new church. The transitions and pressures of life and ministry with a young family were beginning to feel overwhelming. I felt exhausted, misunderstood, frustrated, discouraged, and near the end of my rope. I wanted to quit. For the first time in my adult life, I wanted to do anything but ministry.

I was sharing all of this with my amazing wife one night, and finally in frustration I stood up from the couch and began to stomp around the living room like a toddler, saying, "God, it feels like you are being completely quiet right now! Where are you? I could really use a message from you. Just tell me what I'm supposed to do here!"

I plopped back on the couch and threw my feet up on the coffee table. My wife said, "You've got something stuck on your foot."

I looked down, and there was a sticker on my heel. It must have been left on the floor by one of my kids. As I peeled it off to look at it, I had to catch my breath. I was (and still am) convinced that sticker on my foot was as clear a message from God as I have ever received. It simply read, "KEEP GOING!"

That marked a turning point in my attitude and my perspective. I wrote the date "6–30–10" on that sticker and placed it on the front page of my Bible as a constant reminder. God gave me the strength to press through that difficult season, and very quickly, almost every area of life and ministry began to improve.

KEEP GOING UNTIL YOU REACH THE FINISH LINE!

We've all had moments where we've felt like giving up and moments where we've wondered where God is in all of it. Maybe you're in one of those moments right now in your marriage, your work, or life in general. I pray that you are reminded that God is with you, he is for you, he will carry you through the struggle, he will bring purpose from your pain, and he will reward your faithfulness. Just don't give up. The legacy of love he is creating in and through your life is just getting started. Keep going until you reach the finish line!

> *"And let us run with endurance the race God has set before us. We do this by keeping our eyes on Jesus, the champion who initiates and perfects our faith" (Heb. 12:1–2).*

ACKNOWLEDGMENTS

I am one blessed dude.

First off, I'd like to thank *you* for reading this book. Thank you for investing your time to grow your capacity to give and receive love. It's the most worthwhile of pursuits. I hope the words you've read will be an ongoing source of encouragement in your relationships. Not only did you read the book, but you're actually reading the acknowledgments, which is basically extra credit, so give yourself an extra pat on the back.

God has given me a wonderful partner and best friend in my wife, Ashley. I love you, sweetie! You make me a better person, and I love being your husband. You are an amazing wife and mommy. I can't wait to see what God has in store for us in the years ahead. Next to God's grace, your love is the greatest gift in my life.

God has given me four adorable little boys who bring such joy and light into my life. I love you Cooper, Connor, Chandler, and Chatham! I can't wait to see what amazing plans God has in store for each of you. I'm so honored to be your dad. I love you so much.

God gave me a mom and dad who always displayed what genuine faith and love look like. Words cannot express my gratitude to you both. I'm so thankful for your love and continued support. I still want to be like you guys when I grow up! I love you both.

I'm so thankful for Bill and Mary who are more than just in-laws but have adopted me into their family. My life is richer because of your love and friendship.

I'm so thankful for our siblings: Ben and Anne, Joe and Morgan, Drew and Erin, and their precious kids. Life is much more fun because of you guys!

God has blessed my family with an amazing church home. Stevens Creek Church is a wonderful place to do life. I'm so thankful for the love of an awesome church family, extraordinary friends, and the partnership of an amazing staff team. You guys rock.

Thank you to our small group for sharing your friendship, your prayers, and your best dessert recipes with us.

A very special thanks to my friend and mentor, Dr. Marty Baker, who has given me countless opportunities to grow, lead, and serve. Your impact in my life is immeasurable. Also, thank you for not firing me when I threw a fake funeral for you.

Special thanks to the world's best literary agent, Amanda Luedeke, for believing in this project and the team at Thomas Nelson for bringing it to life. I'm honored to be in partnership with you.

Thanks to Jessica Wong, Heather Skelton, and Katherine

Rowley, whose brilliant insight throughout the editing process made this book much better than it would have been and also made me sound much smarter than I actually am.

Thank you to Katy Boatman, Chad Cannon, Stephanie Tresner, and Tiffany Sawyer for your tenacious work to promote the message of this book and for enduring my endless e-mails and text messages.

Thank you to Shaunti Feldhahn for adding your profound wisdom to the foreword of this book. I'm honored to have your partnership on this project.

Special thanks to John and Jean Kingston, Nancy French, and the team at SixSeeds for your continued encouragement and support of my writing. Ashley and I are so appreciative of the opportunities you've made possible for us.

Thank you to our friends and ministry partners at the Patheos Family Channel, Sword & Spoon Group, XXXchurch.com, The Church of God, Christ's Church Fleming Island, Happy Wives Club, Fierce Marriage, WAFJ Radio, LeadBravely.org, GraceChristian. tv, Augusta Christian Schools, Family Dynamics Institute, OneBigChurch.com, Fireproof Ministries, TruthWebDesign.com, Compassion International, and all our other ministry partners for your continued encouragement and support in our shared efforts to build stronger marriages and families.

I also want to say a heartfelt thank-you to the countless people who have shaped this book and shaped my life through their love. I have many more friends than I deserve!

Thank you to the thousands of encouragers who have reached out to Ashley and me through our websites and live events. Your prayers and support give us strength.

Most important . . . thank you, Jesus! Thank you for your endless grace and limitless love. It's all for your glory!

ABOUT THE AUTHOR

Dave Willis is a husband, dad, pastor, writer, encourager, and ice cream addict. He is the founder of www. StrongerMarriages.org, which has a total weekly reach in the millions. When he's not writing or speaking at conferences and churches across the country, he's usually hanging out with his wife and best friend, Ashley; wrestling with one of their four sons; or working with the extraordinary team at Stevens Creek Church. Dave also spends approximately one thousand hours annually searching for Band-Aids, matching socks, and lost remote controls. He lives in Evans, Georgia. You can find more resources from Dave at www.DaveWillis.org.